Bird Watching
for
Everyone

Bird Watching
for
Everyone

Hockley Clarke

Gresham Books

GRESHAM BOOKS
Unwin Brothers Limited
The Gresham Press
Old Woking
Surrey GU22 9LH

ISBN 0 905418 30 1

First published 1973
New revised edition 1979

Typeset by Reproprint
Leatherhead, Surrey.
Printed in Great Britain by
Unwin Brothers Limited
The Gresham Press
Old Woking
Surrey GU22 9LH

CONTENTS

Appendixes

INTRODUCTION

BIRDWATCHING for everyone! Why not? Some feature of bird life must appeal to you; consider just a few aspects.

This book differs from most others of the many published on the subject in recent years. It is not a field guide, and it does not list species in scientific order. It is helpful on indentification, and its main feature is a concise and unfolding story of bird life as it progresses over the year.

As such, it is a basic study, an introduction to bird life based on lectures given by the author to classes at Adult Educational Centres and elsewhere. It is an orderly, informative, and helpful presentation of birds, their characteristics, their movements, and their varied and fascinating activities, especially during the breeding season.

There is more in bird watching than ticking off new species seen, satisfactory though this is, and to know about them, as this book reveals, brings pleasure and reward to this healthy and inexpensive hobby, which many have found has given them a new interest, a new impetus, beyond their expectations.

Colour: birds are beautiful and those which are not magnificently plumed still have feathers with attractive markings, streaks, spots, and pencilling, set to pattern in each species.

Song: this is so varied that there is something to please the most unmusical of us.

Flight: this is distinctive in each species, with flocks, formations, movement, and migration as related factors.

Nests: these are often exquisitely built and wonderfully varied, from species to species, in style and construction.

Eggs: they come in many shades and tints, spots and streaks, large and small, each distinctive to its species.

However busy we are, or preoccupied with other affairs, a few minutes occasionally can be spared to look at the birds around us — in gardens, parks, the countryside, on inland waters, and at the coast. We cannot fail to notice the variety of bird life, the different types of bird commonly seen, and the habits of birds around us. Birds are a blessing to the human race, no less. Imagine a world without them, and if we look and listen we enrich our lives. Looking at birds opens up new prospects, season by season, as interesting changes take place in plumage, behaviour, and movements. Charles Darwin records that when a young man he first read *The Natural History of Selborne* by Gilbert White, and he wondered why every gentleman in England was not an ornithologist.

We do not have to be ornithologists in the strict meaning of the word to derive pleasure and satisfaction from observing bird life as we pursue our daily activities. This book is designed to help the layman, student, or anyone with an awakening interest in bird life to appreciate the extent of the subject and the potential of bird study as a hobby. It suggests ways of going about it, and what birds can be seen. Many commonly seen species are included and illustrated and there are several appendixes, including a quiz, to help the reader in further pursuit of the subject.

Confining information to the more essential species does not detract from the usefulness of the book, bearing in mind its object and scope. It means that it is not burdened with descriptive detail on birds which are not likely to be seen, or at the most, once or twice in a life time.

It is desired to thank those who have contributed photographs which are such an attractive feature of the book. The contributors are named individually with the photographs.

H. C.

CHAPTER ONE

BASIC BIRD WATCHING

WHETHER or not you are conscious of it, you are already a bird watcher of sorts. Every time you step into the garden or go out of doors you cannot avoid seeing or hearing birds. In city, town, or countryside you will see bird life of some sort – starlings on the lawn, sparrows in the street, or a blackbird in the hedgerow for instance. Quite young children soon learn the names of the common birds which they see every day in the garden or from their window. Most of us make a more detailed acquaintance with the subject at school, during nature study lessons, and even in leisure hours, far away from academic influence. Few can fail to have seen or heard the many admirable television or radio programmes which deal with aspects of bird life, often in considerable depth.

Bird watching – or ornithology if you like – has the rare advantage in this day and age of being virtually a free pastime. It has no special strings attached, no diplomas or examinations to pass, and you can approach it as you like, taking into account only the common rules of decency, the law of the land, and a respect and care for nature. Bird watching can become a major hobby, and you can get fully engrossed in it accordingly. It can become the subject of specialised study – with research, recording, and photography as allied activities – and there are societies, study centres, and courses of various kinds all available for those who wish to make ornithology or bird watching a major hobby. By the same token bird watching can be the most casual of your pastimes, at its simplest merely adding interest to your gardening activities, country walks, or afternoon strolls. Identifying the species you see around you, noting or recognising their characteristics purely for your own interest can be the total extent of your involvement. Between these two extremes you can take the study of the subject to any level you like. Young readers of this book may, indeed, already be studying birds in some depth at school and may already be keeping a 'spotting log' and notes as part of a school project.

For others, perhaps many years past school age, similar activities may be just part of a relaxing hobby. In short, how you develop your interest in bird watching is entirely your affair; buy lots of books, magazines, bird-song records and so on if you wish, or buy none at all – how engrossed you become in bird watching activities is entirely up to you.

What this book aims to do is provide some basic background information of value to amateur bird watchers and embryo ornithologists. It is almost entirely non-scientific in its approach – there is hardly a Latin name to be seen, for instance! – and it is written in layman's terms. It mentions only the more common or better known species in any detail, those you are actually likely to see (depending on where you live) rather than the more exotic species which even a specialist might see only once or twice in a lifetime. The species mentioned are those to be seen in Great Britain, though most are common to much of North West Europe.

This is not a specialised bird recognition book – there are plenty already available – though you can, of course, identify birds from this book by reference to the illustrations and descriptions. This is essentially a book of bird 'lore' which will, I hope, enable you to appreciate more readily the habits, life style, and characteristics of birds, and the environmental factors which influence bird life. The book should help you to look for birds, find conditions amenable to bird watching, and generally help you to be a better bird watcher. At the end of the book the appendixes include a quiz and details of places in Britain where there are special bird sanctuaries or well-known bird-watching amenities.

Before proceeding further, however, a word about how to observe birds would be appropriate. Birds in normal circumstances are harmless to humans and even the most brazenly 'domesticated' of wild birds, like House sparrows are relatively timid and shy as every child learns at a very early age when he runs over to them to make friends! If you want to observe birds, say, while on a country walk, or even in your garden, quiet unhurried movement is naturally a vital necessity. If you wish to look at a bird which has alighted some way ahead of you it is relatively easy to 'freeze' from a slow walk, with no sudden movement of the limbs or body to catch the birds attention. There may be time to move quietly and gently to a new vantage point for a prolonged period of observation without catching the bird's eye. For similar reasons, sober clothing is preferable to garish colours or prominently patterned outer garments. Plain sweaters, shirts, or anoraks are ideal – depending, of course, on the time of year. Incidentally, this

An unusually close view of a female Stonechat. (F. Sanderson Dolley).

Above: *Heavily illustrated field guides, with colour illustrations and full details of all species are an essential aid to bird-watching. Get at least one of the smaller format volumes. Here are just two of the many available.* **Below:** *As well as the typical field guides shown, you can get records of bird song and sets of colour slides (with accompanying notes) by Woodmansterne, for home projection.*

advice about movement and sober colours holds true even if you are observing garden birds from inside the house. Sudden movement or bright colours will still be visible to the bird through the window. If none of this has occurred to you before, try it on your next country walk. Blundering along a footpath trampling twigs and leaves loudly underfoot will drive off all the birds for a long distance in front of you. By contrast, the quiet approach, perhaps with a five-minute stop from time to time – to 'look and listen' – will start to reveal a surprising amount of bird activity going on quite close by.

If your enthusiasm develops further there are several basic aids to bird watching which should be to hand. The first of these, which indeed you may already have, is a good bird recognition book. This is the sort of handy-size volume small enough to carry around, say in your coat pocket or bag, so that any species you wish to identify can be readily turned up on the page. Usually these books illustrate the bird in colour and give basic notes on the species either with the illustration or on an adjacent page. Most of the books, incidentally, contain a vast amount of additional material on the subject of bird watching or identification. Quite apart from assisting positive identification of a species, these books can provide instant information on a bird you may well be able to identify but then wish to confirm or know more about. There are too many bird recognition books to list them all – your local bookshop will almost certainly be able to offer you a choice of several.

Some keen bird watchers buy more than one book of this type. It is a good idea to have one book permanently in your car (if you have one), another for your pocket or bag, and perhaps another in your bookshelves at home.

There is another book, *The Natural History of Selborne,* by Gilbert White (1720-1793), already referred to in the Introduction. It is a delightful book. Read his first-hand observations on the swift and nightjar, and, in particular, the chapter – *Observations on Birds,* a mine of information on many species.

If you do not possess a copy of the book, your local library is likely to have it.

Following on from actually identifying the birds, another activity which can be most interesting – especially after several years of use – is a 'spotting log' where you can record details of the birds you see. At its simplest this can be a spiral-bound notebook (again small enough to go in your pocket or bag) with the pages ruled off in columns and headed as illustrated on the next page.

Copy the sample page exactly if you wish, or vary it to suit yourself. Clearly it is not practical (unless you are, perhaps, retired or on holiday) to keep this 'spotting log' as a daily activity. Some people simply take them on a week-end country walk or use them solely to record birds seen in the garden. It is an entirely optional activity but it can become quite absorbing when the 'logs' of several years are compared, date for date. New species may suddenly appear in your locality, migration dates may differ appreciably if the weather is specially fine or bleak, and these and other happenings which you might observe and then just forget, can be very usefully logged for later reference. On a rather grander scale 'logging' activities not very different from this, but by learned or scientific bodies have contributed over the years to a surprisingly big proportion of what we know today about birds.

DATE	SPECIES	PLACE	NUMBER SEEN	REMARKS
2.5.79	Mistle Thrush (M?)	Garden	1	Hammering snail on stone
4.5.79	Chaffinch (F)	Memorial Park	1	Gathering nest-building materials

Sample page of a 'spotting log' ruled off in a note book.

An essential accessory for bird watching is, of course, a pair of binoculars. Many bird watchers use an old pair which may have been in the family for years. However, if you are buying new, size 8 × 30 is a handy compact size affording clarity and a good field of view. If you shop wisely there is an ample choice available at reasonable modest prices but beware the false economy of buying a cheap optically unsatisfactory instrument. Larger types are available but they are, of course, heavier and usually more expensive.

Bird watching, it its simplest form, can start in your garden. Putting out scraps for the birds is a common household practice, especially in the winter months. A bird table (sited to be inaccessible to cats), or a nesting box, if your garden is big enough, will also attract birds into the garden, and more details on this aspect of the subject can be found in Chapter 8. Living in a country area may give you the opportunity to see a wide range of species in your garden alone, and even town gardens get a surprising number of different species in the course of a year – as, in fact, your 'spotting log' will tell you when you go back through it.

The House sparrow is one of the commonest of all wild birds; this is the male.

Bird 'hides' are often written about and these have valid uses, of course, for serious ornithologists and those engaged in bird photography. The average or casual bird watcher is not likely to reach the stage where he would get involved in building hides, though I have known it done even in the garden where the owner wished to observe the goings on of a nesting family. If you do build a hide, keep it simple. Bean sticks covered with canvas or tenting material make a satisfactory structure, but the sticks must be secured well – embedded in the ground and lashed in a framework – so that the whole lot does not collapse in a breeze. Make the access on the side away from the birds you wish to observe and enter and leave slowly and quietly. It may be several days before the birds get used to the hide's presence and you may also find you need much patient waiting before you actually see anything worthwhile.

CHAPTER TWO

CLASSES OF BIRDS

BIRDS ARE indicated as coming within general descriptive categories, or classes which are summarised below.

Residents are species which remain in the British Isles throughout the year, but there are inland movements, mostly temporary to different parts of the country, and largely determined by seasonal influences.

Summer Visitors are species which arrive in Britain from their warmer winter quarters overseas, roughly from mid-March to early in May. They come to breed, often occupying their former territories, and they depart at varying times, returning to their winter habitats. A few of these summer visitors occasionally winter in Britain, examples being the Reed bunting and the Chiff-chaff.

Winter Visitors come in the autumn mostly from northerly latitudes, and remain during the cold months, examples being the Redwing, Fieldfare, Great grey shrike, Whooper swan, etc.

Passage Migrants are those which we see while they are journeying through territory in which they do not intend to stay; thus they are liable to pass twice a year on their inward and outward journeys. They provide opportunities for seeing uncommon and rare birds not normally expected in the habitat.

Partial Migrants are species which may be both resident and migrant, mostly the former, moving into different territories at various times of the year. For instance, there is a movement of the Song thrush from the north to the south in the winter.

Vagrant is the term for an uncommon or rare bird, a casual visitor.

It follows that these are not rigid categories but they are regarded as descriptive of the normal behaviour of the species.

Omnalia denotes a species in which there are individual birds which belong to all four categories of Winter visitors, Summer visitors, Passage migrants, and Partial migrants.

There are a number of notable features arising from the categories into which the various species fall. For instance, there

Above: *Canadian goose and young on the Thames at Mill End, near Henley. (Raymond Lea).*

Below: *Common sandpiper and young at the nest. (J. S. Simons).*

The Snowy owl is one of the rarer sights for a bird watcher. (F. Sanderson Dolley).

may be changes from winter to summer plumage and vice versa, with an 'eclipse' (or half-way) phase in ducks at the end of the breeding season.

Also there are vast differences in a bird's life during the long hours of daylight in spring and summer, and the few hours of daily activity in the winter which involve slow, but marked, bodily adjustments. These may be noticed in appearance, gait, apparent size, activity, or flight patterns. In fact the behaviour and movements of birds can vary at all times under changing seasonal and other climatic conditions.

A feature of the summer migrants is the punctuality with which they arrive each year, a matter of a day or two's variation at most, according to location. Departure is more haphazard, depending mostly on late broods, and the development of the season's young. For example the adult cuckoos migrate around the end of July, leaving their young behind, while the main body of the swifts depart about the middle of August.

The Woodcock is found in wooded areas keeping shyly hidden during the day and feeding mainly at night. Barred brown plumage assists in concealment.

CHAPTER THREE

SPECIES OF BIRDS

THERE ARE over 400 species on the British list, but less than 100 are the more common or well-known. Below is a selection most important to the average bird watcher, omitting uncommon, or rare birds, which may not be seen in a life time. This list divides into resident species, some of which are augmented by seasonal movements; summer visitors, with a few wintering birds, ie, avocet, reed bunting, chiff-chaff; winter visitors; and passage migrants. There is considerable over-lapping.

Avocet
Arctic tern
Barnacle goose
Barn owl
Bar-tailed godwit
Berwick swan
Black-tailed godwit
Black-necked grebe
Bittern
Blackbird
Blackcap
Black guillemot
Black tern
Black-headed gull
Black-throated diver
Blue tit
Brambling
Brent goose
Bridled guillemot
Bullfinch
Buzzard

Canada goose
Carrion crow
Chaffinch
Chiff-chaff
Chough
Cirl bunting
Coal tit
Collared dove
Common guillemot
Common gull
Common sandpiper
Common scoter
Common tern
Common whitethroat
Coot
Cormorant
Corn bunting
Corncrake
Curlew
Cuckoo
Curlew sandpiper

Dartford warbler
Dipper
Dunlin
Dunnock
Eider
Fieldfare
Firecrest
Gadwall
Gannet
Garden warbler
Garganey
Glaucous gull
Great-crested grebe
Great grey shrike
Great Northern diver
Greylag goose
Goldcrest
Goldeneye
Goldfinch
Goosander
Grasshopper warbler
Greenshank
Greater Black-backed gull
Greater-spotted woodpecker
Greenfinch
Green sandpiper
Green woodpecker
Grey wagtail
Guillemot
Hedge sparrow (Dunnock)
Hen-harrier
Heron
Herring gull
Hobby
Hooded crow
House martin
House sparrow
Iceland gull
Ivory gull
Jackdaw
Jay
Kestrel
Kingfisher

Landrail
Lapwing
Lesser Black-backed gull
Lesser spotted woodpecker
Lesser whitethroat
Linnet
Little grebe
Little gull
Little ringed plover
Little stint
Little tern
Long-tailed duck
Long-tailed tit
Magpie
Mandarin duck
Mallard
Manx shearwater
Marsh tit
Mistle thrush
Meadow pipit
Montagu harrier
Moorhen
Muscovy duck
Mute swan
Nightingale
Nightjar
Nuthatch
Osprey
Oystercatcher
Pied flycatcher
Pied wagtail
Pink-footed goose
Pintail duck
Purple sandpiper
Quail
Raven
Razorbill
Red-breasted merganser
Redpoll
Redshank
Red-throated diver
Redstart (Common)
Redwing

Reed bunting
Reed warbler
Ring ouzel
Ringed plover
Robin
Rock pipit
Red-backed shrike
Roseate tern
Rook
Sanderling
Sand martin
Sandwich tern
Scaup
Sedge warbler
Shag
Shellduck
Shoveller
Siskin
Slavonian grebe
Smew
Snipe (Common)
Snipe (Jack)
Snow bunting
Song thrush
Sparrow hawk
Spotted flycatcher
Starling
Stonechat
Stone curlew
Swallow
Swan (Mute)
Swan (Berwick)
Swift
Tawny owl
Teal
Tree-creeper
Tree pipit
Tree sparrow
Tufted duck
Turnstone
Turtle dove
Velvet scoter
Water rail
Waxwing
Wheatear
Whimbrel
Whinchat
White wagtail
Whooper swan
Widgeon
Willow tit
Willow warbler
Woodlark
Woodpigeon
Wood sandpiper
Wood warbler
Wren
Wryneck
Yellow hammer
Yellow wagtail

Above: *A buzzard in the Highlands of Scotland in mid-winter. (W. Kenneth Richmond).*

Below: *A Great northern diver at Axbridge, Somerset. (Robin Williams).*

Above: *Swallow feeding young in a typical nest built inside an outhouse.*

Opposite: *Great spotted woodpecker about to enter nest. (F. Sanderson Dolley).*

Below: *Wood sandpiper feeding in the shallows on a mudflat.*

Above: *Meadow Pipit seen in the garden. (Robin Williams).* **Below left:** *Sedge warbler.* **Below Right:** *The hoopoe is a rare visitor occasionally seen in the South of England. (S. Greenwood).*

THE NAMES OF BIRDS

An international naming of birds was compiled by Linneas in 1758, and there have been adaptations. Some of these names, popularly known as Latin names, are derived both from the Latin and the Greek.

The birds are arranged in Orders and Families, ie, groups, such as *Galliformes* (game birds), *Charadriidae* (plovers), *Antidae* (ducks, geese, and swans).

Further divisions are Genus and Species. Sometimes there is a sub-species. Thus there may be two or three words for the same bird. These names are printed in italics in most bird books and other ornithological publications, and form a kind of international language.

Examples are:

Wagtails: Family *Montacilladae;* genus *Montacilla.*
Species:
Pied wagtail *(Montacilla alba).*
White wagtail *(Montacilla alba alba).*
Grey wagtail *(Montacilla cinerea).*
Yellow wagtail *(Montacilla flava).*
Blue-headed wagtail *(Montacilla flava flava).*

Sparrows: Family *Polceidae;* genus *Passer.*
Species:
House sparrow *(Passer domesticus).*
Tree sparrow *(Passer montanus).*

Note: The Hedge sparrow, a popular name only, is not a true sparrow but belongs to the family *Prunellidae (Prunella modularis).* It is also known as the Dunnock and the Hedge accentor. This is a good example of how the popular name can mislead the unwary. The clue to the species is in the Latin family name.

The Common gull *(Larus canus)* is not as common as its name suggests. It is scattered around the coasts, and it comes inland to reservoirs and sewage farms. Sometimes small parties are seen, and occasionally a flock of some size but it is not a common bird as is the Black-headed gull and the Herring gull. Perhaps the species was more numerous in years gone by to give rise to the name. This is another instance where a name can mislead. The Hedge sparrow (already noted) is not a true sparrow but those without a discerning eye saw in it some resemblance to the hen House

House sparrow feeding its young.

sparrow, and it was common in gardens, so a suitable name for it seemed to be hedge sparrow.

We have the 'Lesser' whitethroat, but the larger bird is not known as the 'Greater' but 'Common' whitethroat. Then there is the Great Reed warbler, which is now a rare species, but we have not got a 'Lesser' reed warbler, being content to call the smaller and common species just the Reed warbler. The Oystercatcher rarely sees an oyster. He feeds on mussels, cockles, and limpets. He might well have been known as the Musselcatcher, but perhaps Oyster sounded a more select name.

LOCAL NAMES

Many familiar species, and some less familiar, are given local names, often picturesque with an obvious association. In other instances the connection is not clear. However, there is usually a link to be found for the attachment of the name to the bird – a line of enquiry which is rewarding to pursue for those with the time and the inclination to give to it. Bird names and local bird lore are subjects of much interest.

The Chaffinch has about thirty-five local, or nick-names, varying according to counties, or districts, examples being Pink, Daffinch, and Twiggyfinch.

The Yellowhammer has over thirty other names, such as Yellow Bunting, Writing or Scribbling lark, Cheeser, Yellow Yowling, and Bessie Bunting.

The Green woodpecker has forty-seven other names, including Yaffle, Rainbird, Galley (merry) bird, Yaffingale, Woodchuck.

The Whitethroat has over thirty – Nettle creeper, Hedge-chicken, Small Straw, Whishie, being examples.

The Nightjar has twenty-five names – Churn owl, Goatsucker, Eve Jar, Puck bird, Moth owl.

The same applies to many other species on the British list.

Wildfowlers have their names for birds, and falconers special terms which they use; there are the collective nouns applicable to species, such as – a charm of Goldfinches, a watch of Nightingales, a parcel of Oystercatchers, a rookery of Penguins, a raft for a flock of swimming birds, and many others.

DIFFERENCES WITHIN SPECIES

Sea birds are not wholly confined to the sea. Some species come inland to breed. Many gulls have now adapted themselves to a largely inland existence. A large group of birds not strictly sea or land birds; some species are a mixture of both, such as grebes and ducks. Into which category birds mainly fall is determined by their physical characters and features which have evolved to enable them to maintain themselves in the type of environment to which they resort. Thus evolution has equipped all kinds of birds to take advantage of all kinds of conditions in the artic, equatorial, and temperate zones of the earth, and a stimulant is produced in migrating species to trigger off mobility at different times of the year.

It follows that the geological character of any area indicates many of the species that are likely to be found there. Thus when the topography is known it is possible to write down in advance to some extent the kinds of birds expected to be seen there, and a list can be checked off in due course, noting absent species, and perhaps adding one or two not anticipated. As one's experience grows so does the accuracy with which such a list can be compiled. This is interesting because it is an indication of your bird watching progress.

Population counts have been a feature of recent years, and they have provided much valuable information about the movements and numbers of birds – the fluctuations in species in an area. To try and count large numbers can be confusing at first but experience, and a technique, makes this easier, and reasonably accurate. You can do this for your own interest or, better still, take part in some of the counts organised by the national, county, or local organisations.

At any favourable estuary, or mud flats, there may be seen an impressive variety of birds, chiefly waders. They arrive as the tide begins to recede, leaving behind as it slowly ebbs a rich harvest of animal foods in the wet mud and sand. It is there in abundance and great variety, though not visible to the observer, and it is replenished with each incoming and outgoing tide. At such places much can be learnt from the feeding pattern of the birds. Competition is not so intense as it might appear to be because length of legs and length of beaks, and different structures, enable the area to be combed thoroughly. The shallow and deeper pools, with surface creatures, and those below the surface, are all within reach of hungry birds.

The Turnstone is one of the birds whose popular name is descriptive of its activities and it can be seen on coasts and estuaries. It is a passage migrant.

CHAPTER FOUR

AIDS TO IDENTIFICATION

MUCH OF THE FUN and interest in bird watching is, of course, in identifying the species, differentiating between male and female, fledgeling and adult, or even identifying the bird from clues like an abandoned nest or broken eggs. Your sighting of the bird may be of only a fleeting nature, or you may for the first time ever see a bird which is familiar enough to you from pictures in books but which you had never previously sighted. Who, for instance, has ever experienced the thrill of suddenly seeing a completely unusual bird appear among the sparrows and tits on a bird table? You may come across a species of bird new to you, without actually sighting it, for you may merely hear its song for the first time. For instance nearly everyone must have heard the trilling of a Skylark way above the meadows but relatively few of us ever get a really close view of the bird itself. With your bird recognition book to hand, identifying the species is, in theory, easy enough. But you may still have to thumb through the book, you may have had only a brief glimpse of the bird itself, and you may have left the book behind or in the car! So to a greater or lesser extent you may have to depend on memory even to look up the species. With this in mind here is a check list of the points on which to make a special mental note when you see and wish to identify an unfamiliar bird.

Body features
(1) size of body; outline; stance.
(2) colour and character of beak, ie, pointed = mainly insect-eater; thick or heavy = mainly seed-eaters; hooked = bird of prey.
(3) colour and length of leg.
(4) eye-stripe, light or cream/white.
(5) Legs, short or long compared with body; tail, forked, fish-like, or rounded at end.
(6) conspicuous colour markings, spots, eye-stripes, wing bars, streaks.

Bills

Differences indicate feeding habits, food and the type of territory.
Examples are:

Up-turned: Avocet (markedly), Bar-tailed godwit (slightly), Greenshank.

Down-curved: Curlew, Whimbrel, Dunlin, Ruff, Tree-creeper.

Spear shaped: Heron, Kingfisher, Great-crested grebe, Snipe, Sandpipers.

Stout (conical): House sparrow, finches, some buntings, seed eaters.

Hook bills: Birds of prey, ie, hawks, harriers, eagles, owls, shrikes.

Slender: Hedge sparrow, larks, pipits, warblers, insect eaters.

Knob on bill: Mute swan, Shellduck, Common scoter.

Tubular: Fulmar, Razorbill.

Serrated: Goosander, mergansers.

Spatulate: Shoveller.

Peculiarities: Hawfinch – heavy bill; Spoonbill, Crossbill – names indicate.

Legs

Red or pink: Gulls – Black-headed, Herring, Little, Greater Black-backed, Redshank, Arctic tern.

Black or dark: Crows (except Chough), flycatchers, redstarts, shrikes, Pied and Yellow wagtails, Wheatear, Whinchat, Waxwing, Dunlin, Snow bunting.

Orange or yellow: Lesser Black-backed gull, Dartford warbler, Bean and White fronted geese, Cuckoo, Ring plover, Turnstone, Purple sandpiper, hawks (not Osprey); Little tern.

Greenish: Moorhen, Common gull, Common sandpiper, Great-spotted wood-pecker, Greenshank.

Feathers on legs: House martin, Tawny owl, Little and Snowy owls, Red grouse, Ptarmigan, Capercaille, Sparrow hawk.

Long legs: Spoonbill, Heron, Crane, Stork, Egret, Black-winged stilt, Redshank, Greenshank, Bar-tailed godwit, Black-tailed godwit, Curlew, Whimbrel.

Crests, Tufts, Streamers

Crests: Waxwing, Crested tit, Lapwing or Peewit, Hoopoe, Shag more marked in breeding season, Skylark, Short-toed lark.

Tufts: Tufted duck, Red-necked grebe, Great crested grebe, Common heron, Purple heron, Little grebe, Merganser, Goosander.

Streamers: Night heron, Swallow (outer tail feathers).

Pronounced eye-stripe: Sedge warbler, Redwing, Red-legged partridge, Woodlark, Dotterell, Rock pipit, Tree-creeper, Wheatear, Cirl bunting.

The Swallow is easily identified by the streamers formed by its outer tail feathers and by its distinctive style of mud nest.

Nests

Here are just a few examples of nest characteristics which give a clue to the type of inhabitant.

Stick nests: Herons, rooks, crows, some birds of prey.

Cup-shaped: Garden and hedgerow birds, bank nesting species.
   Nests in holes may be sub-divided into:

Trees: Woodpeckers (bore), owls, starlings, jackdaws (use natural holes).

In Banks: Sand martin, Bee-eater.

In Burrows: Puffin, Shearwaters.

Mud nests: Swallow, House martin, Song thrush for lining.

Eggs

Those of hole-nesting species, not exposed, mostly lay white or light cream coloured eggs. Those of ground nesting birds are

The Wheatear has a distinctive black eye-stripe and a prominent white rump (from which its name derives in a corrupted form), and is one of the easiest birds to recognise at a glance. It is a summer migrant and has a grey back with black outer wing feathers.

Birds of prey are recognised by their hooked bills and often by their well developed talons. Some have feathered legs.

often heavily camouflaged with spots, streaks, or mottled to blend with surroundings.

Fledgelings

Ground nesting species emerge from the eggs well developed, with feather growth and hard bills, and are able to move about soon after hatching to get into cover as soon as possible.

Hedgerow, and similar birds with less exposed nests, those in holes, and tree-top nesters have helpless young, naked, and taking up to twelve days, or longer, to mature sufficiently to move about and begin to fend for themselves.

The Partridge is a bird of open fields and its young are therefore well developed from birth. This species has a reputation for the tenacious defence of its young against marauders.

SOME CONFUSING BIRDS

Having examined some of the clues to identification I will go on and talk in detail about the identification features of some species and families where there can be confusion for the bird watcher.

These are:

House sparrow and Tree sparrow,
House sparrow (female) and Hedge sparrow,
Carrion crow, jackdaw and rook,
Blue tit and Coal tit: also Marsh tit and Willow tit,

Swallow and House martin.
Grey wagtail and Yellow wagtail,
Chiff-chaff and Willow warbler,
Mistle thrush and Song thrush,
Greater and Lesser Black-backed gulls.

There are other somewhat confusing species, especially in the large group of warblers, waders and coastal species such as the terns. It is desirable to concentrate upon a few species at a time and get their differences clear. We will proceed to do this with the species listed.

Sparrows

The House sparrow *(Passer domesticus)* and the Hedge sparrow *(Prunella modularis)* are different species with different characters and habits. The male House sparrow is unlikely to be confused with the Hedge sparrow. It has a stouter beak (similarly the female) and a black bib, missing in the female. She more resembles the Hedge sparrow, but the marked differences soon become clear.

The Hedge sparrow, or Dunnock, is an unobtrusive bird, keeping generally low down in hedges, bushes, and garden undergrowth. It feeds quietly, and usually alone, or with its mate, rarely taking part in scrambles at the bird table but preferring to wait and peck up any small crumbs, or seeds, left by the others. The Hedge sparrow is neatly patterned brown, with a bluish-grey crown and nape, not very obvious. It has a pointed bill, as do all insect eaters.

The Tree sparrow should be mentioned here, and the differences between this bird and the House sparrow noted. The Tree sparrow is not so common as the House sparrow. It has a chocolate crown and a black spot on each white cheek, and two white wing bars, but its general bodily appearance resembles the House sparrow, though it is slimmer and slightly quicker in its movements.

Crows

The Carrion crow is larger than the jackdaw, and this last is easy to identify by its grey mantle. Both jackdaws and rooks are communal, or social living birds. Not so the Carrion crow, nearly always seen singly or in pairs, except at the end of the breeding season when parties of adults and young remain together for some time.

The plumage of the rook often looks ragged. Its heavy beak and

The Rook with its bald face is as distinctive as its nesting habits, in rookeries high in the trees.

bald face clearly establishes its identity. Mixed flocks of rooks and jackdaws are common.

There is also another species of crow, the Hooded or Grey crow, common in Ireland, less common in Scotland, but less often seen in England. Its ash grey mantle and underparts are clearly seen.

Tits

The Blue tit and the Coal tit are about the same size. The Coal tit is not quite so colourful, and it can be picked out by a white patch on the back of the head and neck.

The Marsh tit (not a true garden species) has a glossy black head; note that the Willow tit is very similar but with a sooty crown.

The Long-tailed tit, an open country bird, is obvious from its long tail.

The calls of these species differ and thus provide a means of identity even when the birds cannot be seen.

Swallow: House martin

The swallow has a chestnut throat, and two long outer tail feathers, known as streamers; the House martin has a white throat, and a fish-like tail. In flight, white is shown around the rump.

Tree Sparrow

Swift

The swift *(apus apus)* is referred to here as with the two species mentioned it is a familiar bird in the summer sky.

The swift cannot be confused, with its long curved wings and short legs, its flickering flight, and torpedo-shaped body. It is not a perching bird. It looks black in the air, but it is really sooty brown.

The nests of these three true birds of the air are interesting and distinctive. The swallow has a cup-shaped nest in a porch or outhouse, the House martin, also a mud nest, plastered to the wall under the eaves, and the Swift which nests out of sight in lofts, attics, or towers, uses little material for its single brood of, usually, two young ones.

Wagtails

Because the Grey wagtail, a resident British species, has a conspicuous area of yellow about it, it is often confused with the

Yellow wagtail which is brown marked above and yellow beneath. The Pied wagtail, a resident species, mainly looks blue-black and white – a quick moving bird, running in short bursts. It needs to be separated from the White wagtail *(Motacilla alba alba)*, a summer visitor. This has a more greyish mantle, and slightly more white on the sides of the head, running into the white breast; white showing on wings and tail. This is a sub-species of the Pied wagtail.

Warblers

Of the summer visitors, the warblers are a varied and important group, quick moving birds, with different songs which they repeat continually. Of these, the Chiff-chaff and the Willow warbler are the most common in many areas. They are difficult to distinguish apart, and their two distinct songs, the first a chirruper and the second a songster, as Gilbert White described them, is the only sure way to identify the birds, except when seen in the hand.

The Chiff-chaff repeats, time and again, 'chiff-chaff, chiff-chaff" The Willow warbler utters a silvery cascade of song, which rises and falls away into a sweet dwindling refrain.

The Grasshopper warbler, small, slim, pale and white underneath, sings during the day as well as by night, with a grasshopper trill, lasting from a few seconds to minutes. The Garden warbler, brown, unbroken by streaks, pale beneath is noted for the long duration and evenness of its phrasing.

The Blackcap, male with black head, female with rufus, utters a loud, liquid and passionate outburst. The Wood warbler begins haltingly and the song develops into a shivering trill, all lasting only a few seconds.

Two Thrushes

The Mistle thrush, or Storm cock, and the Song thrush are very different in appearance, though their songs are not easy to separate until well known. The first is a large, brownish grey looking bird, with a well-spotted breast, something like the Song thrush which is smaller and browner. The Mistle thrush utters a clear, challenging and repetitive song and the Song thrush a more varied song. This latter is a typical garden bird whereas the Mistle thrush likes trees, and more open country. His singing spot is usually at the topmost branch.

The Song thrush and the Redwing are easily confused. The latter is an autumn and winter visitor. The important differences are the pronounced eyestrip in the Redwing and the crimson patch on each flank, not on the wing, as might be assumed from its name.

Finches

The Chaffinch and the Brambling, the first resident, and the second an autumn and winter visitor is therefore only to be seen at these seasons. As the Brambling consorts with Chaffinches, they can often be seen together, and compared in the field, and at close range. The double bar of white on the wings of the Chaffinch, and white on the outer tail feathers is a useful indication, separating it from the Brambling with its white rump, orange shoulder patch and orange on the breast. Other finches are distinctive.

Whitethroats

With the Common whitethroat and the Lesser whitethroat, the latter is a more skulking bird, slightly smaller and overall greyer looking, lacking the chestnut on the Common whitethroat. The Lesser does not indulge in vertical song flights, and the songs of these two birds are different, with a rather scratchy, jerky utterance of the Common variety, while the Lesser begins with a soft warble which is developed into a fairly long running passage.

Curlew and Whimbrel

The first is the largest wader; the second is similar to it but a smaller bird, with bold stripes on the head, missing in the Curlew. Both have long down-curved bills.

Snipe

The Common snipe and the Jack snipe are easily confused. Here again we have a larger and smaller bird, otherwise very similar, using the same type of habitat. The Jack snipe is an autumn and winter visitor, however.

Gulls

The two gulls, the Greater and the Lesser Black-backed, are identified by the larger size of the former, and its black back and flesh coloured legs. The Lesser is about the size of the Herring gull, slatey-grey in place of black, and its legs are yellow. Both these gulls, and the Herring gull, come inland to reservoirs and other enclosed waters.

The Herring gull is slightly larger than the Lesser Black-backed gull, and the general impression is of a white and grey bird. It has a

Snipe.

heavy yellow bill with a red spot on the lower mandible. The legs
are pink. The red spot may be seen by the young as a dark blotch,
and, as such, is a pointer to the food source.

The Black-headed gull *(Larus ridibundus)* is a smaller gull with a
chocolate brown crown in the breeding season. It is larger than
the Little gull *(Larus minutus)* which is rarely seen. This has a black
head, the black running rather deep down the neck, grey wings
and back, and smoky black on the undersides of the wings. In
summer the bill is red and the legs vermilion; in winter it has a
black bill and flesh coloured legs. In winter the black on the head
disappears. The Common gull *(Larus canus)* and the Kittiwake
(Rissa tridactyla) are about the same size, both with white, silver-
grey wings, black on tips; the Common gull has 'mirrors', but not
the Kittiwake. Both have greenish-yellow bills, and the legs of this
gull are greenish in colour while the legs of the Kittiwake are
black.

Three whitish looking gulls are (1) the Glaucous gull *(Larus hyperboreus)* which is about Herring gull size, with whitish grey back and wings and flesh coloured legs. This is a scarce winter visitor to Scottish coasts, east England, and west Ireland; (2) the Iceland gull *(Larus glauciodes)* has plumage similar to the Glaucous gull but is a smaller bird, with wings conspicuously reaching beyond the tail when at rest; (3) the Ivory gull *(Pagophila eburnea)* is small and white, with dark legs, suffused pink on breast and bill black to yellow with red tip. It is a winter vagrant.

A typical small wader is the Ringed Plover.

Waders
With the smaller waders, like the Dunlin, Little stint, and Ringed plover (see below), the Larger Knot, Sanderling, Turnstone, and Oystercatcher, and larger waders such as the Redshank and the Greenshank, Godwits, Curlew and Wimbrel, their length of legs and character of beak determines in a general way where they feed on the soft table of mud and water which is laid with delicacies at every ebb of the tide.

The two plovers, the Ringed *(Charadrius hiaticula)* and the Little Ringed *(Charadrius dubius)* are somewhat alike though the latter is the smaller of the two, and can be identified by the yellow orbital ring around the eye. Unlike the Ringed it has no white wing bar. The Little is uncommon, having re-established itself as a British breeding species only since 1945.

Sea Birds

The Cormorant and the Shag are easy to identify but the two may be confused until their differences are known. The Cormorant has a white throat and cheeks, features absent in the Shag. The latter displays a crest more conspicuous during the breeding season. It is slightly smaller than the cormorant.

Cormorants come inland more than Shags, swimming up tidal rivers, and visiting reservoirs. Though black looking, both have green, bronze, and violet reflections in their plumages, more marked in the breeding season.

Parties of Cormorants may be seen standing together on shore, holding out their wings as if to dry them; but this is probably a digestive action after feeding.

Of the Common and Velvet Scoters, the first is an all black bird, the second is black but has two distinctive white features, a small patch of white under the eyes, and a large patch on each wing. This may not be visible when the bird is swimming but the white is conspicuous in flight.

The Common Guillemot and Razorbill are two sea birds which adopt the same upright stance and posture. The Guillemot is slightly the smaller of the two, with a straight, pointed bill whereas the Razorbill has an arched bill (furrowed), with clear white lines.

There are two other species of Guillemot, the Black and the Bridled. The first is smaller than the Common, with red legs and feet, and a bold white patch on the wings in summer, broken by black and white plumage above in winter, and white beneath. The Bridled is not often seen. It has yellow legs, and a white circle around the eye.

Waterfowl

A further group of birds are known as waterfowl. Using the description in its widest sense it includes Britain's three species of swans, the Mute, Whooper and the Berwick, diving ducks such as the Tufted, Goldeneye, Widgeon, and Pochard, Saw-bill ducks like the Goosander and the Smew, grebes and divers.

Swans

Two of the three species of swans mentioned are much alike but distinctive from the third – the Mute. The latter is the most common, readily identified by its curved neck and arched wings, a red beak with a black knob at the base. This is a semi-domesticated species, while the other two, the Whooper and Berwicks, are truly wild swans. In both of these the neck is usually held straight. They seldom arch their wings over their backs; both have yellow bills, with areas of black on them. The Whooper shows more yellow than black, and the Berwick, which is smaller than the Whooper, shows more black than yellow.

Ducks

The Pintail, a surface feeding duck, is a resident, a graceful, white-breasted bird, with a white strip running down the neck meeting the white breast. Its head is dark brown and the tail long and pointed, though not so long as that of the Long-tailed duck. These are the only ducks with long tails, and the latter is the smaller of the two.

The Shoveller is unmistakable because of its large spoon-shaped bill. The drake Shoveller is colourful in Spring and in Summer with his beautiful green head, white breast and chestnut flanks, and with black and white on the stern.

Widgeon are numerous. This duck has a high forehead, a handsome chestnut head, a very short bill, and a broad wing bar. The whistling call of the drake, 'Whee-ooo', comes constantly over the water, and tells of the presence of widgeon amongst great rafts of ducks before they can be picked out.

The Goldeneye is a white-looking duck, that is, it has a white breast and underparts which stand out on the water. Its head is green, and there is a large white spot on the cheeks of the male. The plumage on the back is pied.

The Tufted duck is to be seen almost everywhere on reservoirs and park waters, a dark-looking small duck, with oblong patches of white on the flanks. The tuft of feathers at the back of the head is not always raised and visible.

Scaup (*Aythya marila*) has some resemblance to the Tufted duck (*Aythya fuligula*) mainly because the female has a prominent white blaze around the base of the beak and many Tufted ducks show white on the face, though not so extensive as the Scaup duck.

The Scaup is larger than the Tufted. It is a sea duck, occasionally seen inland in the winter. The drake's head, neck, and chest, are black, the back grey, delicately mottled, and it has a white wing bar.

The Teal, the smallest European duck, and fairly numerous, is easily picked out by its chestnut head and the broad green band across it. Also to be mentioned is the Shellduck, a large handsome duck, to be seen on shores, and in estuaries and on mud-flats, looking black and white, and distinguished by the chestnut band encircling the breast and over the back.

Coming to the saw-bill ducks, the Smew is the smallest. These ducks have saw-edged mandibles. The drake Smew is white, very white in water, with black markings around the eye and on the head. The female has a chestnut cap, with white cheeks, dark grey breast and slate grey back.

The Smew, with the Goosander, comes south to inland waters in the winter, as does the Red-breasted merganser. A feature in both the goosander and the merganser is the long blood red, slender bill.

The head of the drake Goosander is dark green, the back black and white, the breast creamy, with white; the flanks and underparts salmon pink flush. The Red-breasted merganser hardly lives up to its name, for its breast is more chestnut than red.

Grebes

In the winter the Great-crested grebe is a dark greyish and white bird often seen out in the middle of a reservoir, with a long body and slender neck, a small flat head. All this changes with the coming of the breeding season when the bird grows ear-tufts and coverts.

The Little grebe, or Dabchick, is a lively, almost tailless bird, as are all the grebes, with, in summer bright chestnut cheeks. It has a short black bill.

Other grebes are the Slovonian, a smaller bird than the Great crested, the Red-necked and Black-necked grebes, with straw feathers back from each eye. The bills are short and slightly upturned. The Slovonian has tufts of chestnut feathers on the side of the head. These three grebes are less common than the Little and the Great-crested grebes.

Divers

The divers frequent Scottish lochs, and inland lakes, but some also winter south, around the Irish coast. They are the Black-throated, the Red-throated, and the Great Northern diver. The Red-throated is the smallest of the three, and the most likely to be seen. Their plumage is beautifully patterned black and white. The Great Northern diver does not breed in Britain.

CHAPTER FIVE

BIRD MIGRATION

MIGRATION IN BIRDS is a purposeful and mysterious force, an
urge that cannot be denied. We tend to think of the migrants as
those birds which come to Britain from long distances for their
breeding season in the spring. This immense influx of birds from
other countries is the most spectacular movement to those who
take notice of it, but it is remarkably unobtrusive to the general
public, considering the number of birds involved. They are widely
distributed, and they settle in their accustomed habitats quietly.

However, the autumn outward-bound migration is another
major movement: also there are movements by resident species
from summer to winter quarters, and there is an inward migratory
movement of birds leaving their summer quarters to winter in
Britain.

Thus with many species such as the Chiff-chaff, Willow warbler,
Swallow etc, their sojourn in Britain is clear-cut, namely, they
arrive, breed and depart. Occasionally, an odd bird or two may
winter in Britain, but these are insignificant to the main stream of
the migratory pattern. The over-all picture is more confused with
familiar species, the Wood pigeon, Starlings, and others which
arrive in the autumn to augment the populations of these resident
species.

Each bird is capable of migrating independently, of finding its
own way, even young birds on migration for the first time; but
when migrating many species tend to flock, and may travel in
small, or large, parties, and sometimes in mixed flocks.

Migration is triggered off by the general fitness of the bird, its
bodily well-being, the putting on of weight and fat as a food source
to draw upon, stimulated by the change in the seasonal weather
pattern. These and other considerations tune up a bird to the point
when it is forced to begin its long, hazardous journey.

Migrating birds tend to move over a wide front, taking
advantage of the more sheltered places in the countryside through
which they have to pass, mountain passes, river valleys, etc, where

A common autumnal sight; Swallows congregating ready to migrate, in this case on a barn roof. Man-made telephone wires offer a similar facility.

it might be expected that there is less wind resistance to their passage. They do not usually continue their journey in head winds, though they may have to do so if the wind changes adversely for them while they are over the sea, and they may be driven to return to the shores which they have left, rather than 'fight' the wind and try to complete the crossing at that time. While their judgment of the best course to pursue may sometimes be at fault, it is an instinctive choice which seems to be naturally pre-determined to ensure the survival of the greatest number. This accords with the survival theory – the paramount consideration in all these migratory movements.

Much migration takes place at night, at varying heights according to climatic conditions. Thus darkness is not an obstacle for this is seldom total, whereas fog, if at all severe, renders flight impossible, or extremely hazardous, for birds air-borne and forced to fly through it.

Three main questions arise:

Why do birds migrate?
When do they migrate?
How do they find their way?

Migration has taken place since the dawn of animal life. Mammals, reptiles, insects, butterflies, and fish migrate as well as birds.

It is held by some that migratory movements have been evolved since the last ice age, but it seems that they are likely to have commenced much earlier. Ice covered and receded from vast areas of the world at different times, with centuries of stability before what we are apt to regard as its final clearance. Thus the patterns of migration, as we know them, have become established over a very long time.

More often heard than seen, the Cuckoo is perhaps the best known of all summer migrants. It has a somewhat hawk-like appearance.

A number of favourable influences occur, and coincide, climatic conditions which make an impact on birds. The sun, light and warmth, begins to return to the western world in the spring. There is a resurgence of growth, new leaves, flowers and insect life, providing cover and food. Thus former territories become available again, places in which birds are able to live, and reproduce their young.

The stream of summer migrants to Britain begins about mid-March with, usually, the arrival of the Wheatear first. In the period following, up to early May many other species arrive, including, of course, the cuckoo and the warblers, with the Spotted flycatcher and the Quail bringing up the rear about the 10-12 May.

The growing light and warmth from the sun draws the birds westward because their biological make-up (hormones) respond to the favourable seasonal influences; therefore, they move instinctively, as countless generations before them have done, to take advantage of new living space which has again been opened up to them.

Why some species migrate and not others depends on adaptability, instinct, and a delicate balance of factors concerning the survival of a species. Migration is a device which enables species to overcome climatic changes and helps to ensure that the population status is maintained, year after year, this despite the heavy mortality to which migrating birds are subject throughout their long journeys, twice annually there and back.

In recent years much new information has been obtained, gleaned from world-wide sources, strategically placed observatories and recording stations, and even radar to track night movements of birds. Sometimes even small transmitters have been attached to birds to track their individual flights. Also many more birds are now ringed, recovered in traps, released, and perhaps recovered at the same place in the following year, and in future years.

In the autumn, as seasonal climatic influences decline, reverse movements take place to those in spring, when migrants leave for warmer countries, equatorial and southern Africa, Spain, and elsewhere.

The Golden oriole is a rare visitor sometimes seen.

Meanwhile other species arrive in Britain from more northerly latitudes to spend the autumn and winter. Familiar ones are the Redwing and the Fieldfare, with a number of others, and there is a southward drift from many areas.

Other spectacular journeys by migrant birds, twice a year as part of their life cycles, are made by a number of species including New World ones. Some make long and hazardous journeys not intentional. For instance, a number of North American birds cross the Atlantic on favourable winds, some settle on ships but the evidence is growing that they are able to make the ocean crossing unaided. These are not authentic migratory movements, but chance visits, though more are being recorded, possibly because there are more discriminating bird watchers now to identify them.

In recent years, unusual species arriving at Cape Clear, off Southern Ireland, in the Scilly Isles and elsewhere have included a northern water thrush, spotted sandpiper, upland (or Bartram's sandpiper, and a red-eyed vireo. Another rare visitor has been the Bobolink from the grasslands of North America. Thus, in passing, it is worth noting that any favourably placed bird-watcher stands a chance of seeing an exotic and unusual species from time to time.

But the vital question remains unanswered concerning our constant migrants. They not only flock southwards and westwards but they return to the same place, the same porch, or outbuilding, the same house, hedge, or tree, where they bred, or where nestlings were hatched the previous year. This points to a fine directional mechanism in each bird. Old birds have made the journey before, but young birds coming back for the first time find their way with equal facility.

SUMMER MIGRANTS

These birds arrive in Britain in the Spring from their Winter habitats overseas, from mid-March to early May, roughly in the order shown, subject to weather conditions and variations occurring dependent upon locality:

Avocet	Wryneck
Wheatear	Tree Pipit
Chiff-chaff	Yellow wagtail
Ring Ouzel	Blackcap
Osprey	Swallow
Willow warbler	House martin
Sand martin	Black redstart

Common redstart   Dotterel
Marsh warbler   Stone curlew
Reed bunting   Whinchat
Sedge warbler   Nightingale
Cuckoo   Corncrafke
Grasshopper warbler   Pied flycatcher
Hobby   Swift
Common whitethroat   Nightjar
Litte-ringed plover   Great skua
Lesser whitethroat   Red backed shrike
Common sandpiper   Spotted flycatcher
Wood warbler   Terns
Garden warbler   Quail
Turtle dove

AUTUMN AND WINTER VISITORS

A few species to see are:
The Redwing, Fieldfare, Jack Snipe, Great-grey Shrike, Brambling, Waxwing.

Nest of Goldfinch.

CHAPTER SIX

COURTSHIP AND DOMESTIC LIFE

BIRD WATCHERS know that is is unwise to be too dogmatic about birds. To say that a species, or an individual bird, does this, or does not do that, is liable to be contradicted by instances that are not true to pattern. We can only write with certainty about established behaviour in considering a species life cycle.

It has been stated that some birds are in possession of territory, established with a mate at the outset of a new breeding season. A few species are known to mate for life. Some migrant species arrive in Britain already mated. Generally however, and with first year birds, allowing that some do not breed until their second year, and one or two species wait until their third year or longer, the procedure is to establish a territory and attract a mate. The cock achieves both these objects by his song. We interpret this as telling intruders to keep out; he says, 'I am in possession here', and he invites a partner to share this territory and to rear a family.

COURTSHIP

When a partner is attracted he has to woo her. Again, song plays a part, and there follows a courtship behaviour, or ritual, which birds undertake in their own special ways. In general, their courtship has marked similarities to that practised by humans in showing attentiveness, the desire of the male to create an impression, even to the extent of putting on a 'best dress'. In this respect, it is the cock bird's finest hour, in vigour and plumage display. Some species are adorned with feathers, a head-dress, crest, or tufts, and assume marks and colours of special significance.

Codes of behaviour and the conduct of each sex assumes a set pattern in each species. In some it is not very obvious, in others it is striking and prolonged, graceful and fascinating. The Great-crested grebe, as is well known, has a wonderful ceremonial courtship ritual, and it has been described in detail in a book by Sir Julian Huxley.

Above: *Nest of a black-headed gull. (P. Thornton).* **Below:** *The nest of a moorhen in the reeds at the riverside.*

Above: *Young Linnets in the nest. (G. Handley).* |**Opposite:** *A Goldfinch high in a horse chestnut tree.* **Inset:** *Reed Warbler in typical surroundings.*

Above: *Shag. (F. Sanderson Dolley).*

Often gifts pass in the course of this courtship procedure, it may be a feather, a straw, or with the grebe mentioned, a water weed presentation charmingly offered.

During the courtship of the Kingfisher, the male offers his mate fish, which she takes and swallows. The prompting and offering of gifts is done to please and impress, the reasons why courting males in the human species offer presents to the object of their devotions.

The bickerings of House sparrows in the early Spring, when several birds suddenly take part in a scramble with a hen bird the centre of attraction is a breeding season preliminary, not graceful, but achieving its object just as effectively as more elaborate displays.

In some species the males make all the 'running', in others, again the grebe, both birds jointly engage in their courtship act.

SITE SELECTION

We have seen that nesting sites conform to the type of habitat peculiar to the species, ie, on or near water, in trees or bushes, in holes in trees, or in banks, etc. It should be pointed out, however, that often unusual nesting sites are chosen, in built-up areas, and sometimes elsewhere, when the territory of a nesting pair does not offer a conventional site. In this respect, some species show more adaptability than others. This means that they can remain in the same breeding territory after it has changed its character, mostly due to alterations made by man.

Where no compromise is possible the birds concerned have to move elsewhere. A Song thrush chose to build a nest in a hole in a wall instead of in a tree, or a hedge, though these were available: House sparrows vacated their nests under the eaves of a house, having been ousted by starlings, and they constructed nests in a cork-oak tree nearby, though good sites for this species were available in adjacent farm buildings.

To us, some nesting sites seem to be unwisely chosen and to invite destruction. Often they survive, and the confidence of the birds in exposing their nesting affairs close to human habitations, or activities, is rewarded because the proximity of people keeps away other predators. Few persons willingly destroy a bird's nest. The energy which they put into building it, and later the devotion of the parents to their young is something that appeals to us, and we want them to succeed.

The selection of a site is instinctive more than anything else as a place suitable for the purpose. This does not, of course, take into

Sand martins nest in sandy banks, actually tunnelling into the sand. They usually nest in small colonies as shown here. Colonies have in recent years been known to nest in drainage pipes above streams.

consideration factors which we, as humans, regard as unfavourable. That there is often a change of plan, a nest commenced and deserted for no apparent reason to us is usually due to outside causes, or influences. Some impact made on the birds causes them to desert the site for a new one, often nearby.

It will be appreciated that through all the developing stages of the nesting story, site selection, laying eggs, incubation, brooding and feeding of young, and when they leave the nest, there are innumerable hazards, including that of the weather, and it is remarkable bearing this in mind that so many young survive to reach maturity, though the mortality rate among them is high.

NESTS

A nest is a place in which eggs are laid, incubated, and in which the young are reared. Consider the nests of plovers, terns, and some other species – ideal nests for them, though they are mere depressions in the ground, plus a few grass bents, or straws. In the open their scanty construction helps them to escape attention. By contrast, nests in cover, hedges, bushes, trees, and grassy banks, are more elaborate, and some are decorative. This decoration is not for a pleasing effect. It is camouflage for security, a means of making a nest blend with its surroundings, again to make it inconspicuous. The nest of the Long-tailed tit is an example, as is that of the chaffinch, both use moss and lichens: both are beautiful nests according to human standards.

Nightingale's nest.

Eagles and their nest.

Herons and rooks with their large nests of sticks in the tops of trees are usually well out of reach and therefore need not be concealed. This enables building to begin before the trees are fully in leaf. Then there are the mud nests of the swallows and the House martins – the first a neat mud-cup built inside an out-house or porch, and the second, usually outside, under the eaves, a complete mud exterior plastered to the wall under the overhanging roof with a small hole at the top to permit entry and exit.

Nest of Song thrush.

In contrast, the swift nests out of sight in church towers, lofts, and caves where a scantily built nest suffices. This also applies to the owls and the woodpeckers; their nests are not visible, but are well protected inside a cavity or a hole.

The Sand martins tunnel into sandy banks, or cliffs, and lay their eggs at the end of it, like those rare visitors to Britain, the Bee-eaters; they came to Sussex and bred in 1957.

These are some of the very different nests, built to meet the needs of the bird in the habitat selected.

Then there are birds such as the grebes. They construct nests made of waterside vegetation, and they cover their eggs with pieces of it when they leave them, if only for a short time, to conceal them from predators.

As a notable example of a nest in a difficult situation that of the Reed warbler, a common summer migrant, is worth mentioning. This is attached to the stems of reeds, and hangs over the water, a deep, cup-like structure made of dead reed stems and other waterside vegetation.

Nest of Yellow hammer.

Nest of House sparrow.

Nest of owl (hole in tree) with fledgelings.

Of British species, only the cuckoo is nest-less, using a foster parent to hatch its eggs and rear its young. Cuckoos lay more than one egg, but each one is in a different nest. Here, too, there is territorial selection in the sense that a pair of cuckoos choose an area to comb for the nests of suitable fosterers to carry out their family duties.

Such nests excite our admiration, so aptly described in the verse of James Hurdis (1763-1831):

> *It was my ambition*
> *To view the structure of that little work*
> *A bird's nest — mark it well, within, without,*
> *No tool had he that wrought, no knife to cut,*
> *No rail to fix, no bodkin to insert,*
> *No glue to join; his little beak was all;*
> *An yet how neatly finished.*

Rooks have a well developed communal sense, many pairs establishing rookeries high in tree-tops; rooks' nests are made quite roughly from sticks.

EGGS

Free ranging creatures like birds, reptiles, insects, and fishes have developed a special reproductive process. This was essential as they could not be hampered by carrying their young about within themselves. Birds being air-borne creatures, lightness and totally unrestricted movement was necessary for their survival. Thus the means had to be devised to ensure an embryo, or life spark, and to provide it with sustenance during development; at the same time it was necessary for the female to discard it, a self-supporting vehicle while being brooded.

The perfect answer to this was the egg, a complicated entity, fragile, yet in itself strong enough to withstand all reasonable pressures. Thus came about also the nest, the place in which the female deposited her eggs, and she became free from the burden of bearing unborn young. Her most onerous duty, sometimes shared by her mate, is to sit on the eggs, the warmth from her body keeping them at the right temperature to ensure the development of the young inside them.

There was still an embellishment to come, namely, the decoration of the shell with shades of colour, blotches, or streaks, which evolved a pattern peculiar to a species, with little variation. This applied mostly to those species which laid visible eggs, as distinct from those of the owls, woodpeckers, and others laid out of sight in holes, cavities, etc, and obscured from view. The colouration of the egg is an aid to comouflage, to make them less noticeable by breaking up the basic colours, so blending better with the surroundings. In some species this is remarkably effective, and is an important protective device. In others, the purpose is not easily appreciated. The Hedge sparrow, for instance, lays a plain, sky blue egg, conspicuous in the nest. Why blue, and why unmarked? Possibly blue is not a colour that is recognised by birds.

Eggs laid in cup-shaped nests, or depressions, are usually elongated, narrowing at one end, and they lie in the nest with the pointed, or narrow end, facing inwards. This prevents the eggs from rolling about and is convenient for the bird to sit on them. This also applies to sea birds whose eggs are laid on cliff ledges, etc. Again, the eggs of owls and other birds which nest in secure holes differ; they are usually round, with no tapering end.

Thus eggs of varying sizes, shapes, and colours, are composite vehicles containing embryo life, the food necessary to nourish it, and a casing to hold it during the process of development of the young bird. The shell casing is reinforced with a tough under-covering of a skin-like substance.

It goes without saying that if you discover a nest by chance, leave it alone and keep away, though by all means observe its position from a distance. It may appear abandoned to you, or it may be occupied by eggs or a nesting pair. Whatever its apparent state, however, the keen bird-watcher will not attempt to tamper with either the nest or the eggs.

INCUBATION AND SANITATION

As a depository for eggs, and as an incubating medium, the inside of the nest must be kept within temperature limits. This is necessary to provide sufficient warmth, but not too much heat, in which the forming chicks can develop and flourish.

To maintain the temperature required inside the nest the warmth generated by the body of the sitting bird is finely controlled. This is achieved by an instinctive process. The duration of a sitting varies with different species. Sometimes outside factors may intervene, the sitting bird my be disturbed, frightened, and kept away from the nest too long, leaving the eggs to get cold. When this happens the life inside them is extinguished. This is more likely to occur than overheating, avoided by the instinctive judgment of the bird. There are species where the bird sits for a surprisingly long period without leaving the eggs, but this is necessary due to the construction of the nest, the size of the egg, and other factors.

There are species, too, in which both the cock and hen birds incubate in alternate sessions, a time-table carried out with remarkable consistency. Thus, left alone, seldom does a bird over-sit or under-sit, so effectively attuned to the end are the responses and urges of the bird.

When incubation is over, and the eggs are hatched, there remains other problems. A major one is that of sanitation. It is not a matter of mere cleanliness. The excrement from the young is composed of chemical substances which in the enclosed structure of the nest would become active, generating heat, and this would be harmful to the chicks. It is removed by the parents. How? The only implements available to them are beak and claws. Here we see a small but vital provision, the enclosing of the excrement in a sac, or bag, a light container which can be easily picked up in the beak, and dropped outside the nest.

The removal of excrement in this ingenious way is necessary only for a short period. Soon the young birds obey another instinctive impulse. They solve the problem themselves by placing their exteriors over the rim of the nest to allow the excrement to fall outside it.

The same nest is sometimes used for a second brood, with some renovation, as necessary, and occasionally for a third brood. Some nests like those of the carrion eaters get fouled, the surrounds littered with bones, and other remains of food brought to the young by their parents who are not meticulous in removing this debris. This may be taken as evidence of a bird's lack of smell. The Kingfisher's nest suffers in this respect by the decaying remains of fish fed to the young. However, they do not seem to be affected by these offensive evidences of their domestic life.

The young of some species more than others (the Swift is an example), get contaminated by parasites which feed on their bodies, often with fatal results.

FLEDGELINGS

Not all young birds emerging from the eggs are naked and helpless. Provision has been made to safeguard their first immaturity, to give them a reasonable chance of survival in a world full of hazards and dangers. For instance, the chicks of ground nesting birds, like pheasants and partridges, are covered with down and immature feathers upon hatching. They see daylight for the first time well clothed. Very soon they can run fast and scramble to cover at the first sign of danger. Similarly equipped to surmount the extra perils from being hatched in exposed positions, the young of species of water birds, coots, moorhens, ducks, etc, can swim expertly on leaving the egg and are, at once, eager, active little creatures in the water. They, too can move to cover when danger arises.

Definitely the parent birds talk to their young in the sense that they make noises, calls, and alarm notes which are understood and acted upon. And even while a chick is in its shell, developed to the point of breaking out by the use of an egg-tooth, conversation goes on between the parent and the as yet unhatched youngster.

In these instances, the need for early mobility has been met. This does not arise similarly with young hatched in nests in cover, like those of the hedgerow and tree nesting birds, screened from view and sheltered by foliage.

Fledgelings grow quickly in favourable conditions, good weather, adequate food, security. The feeding process is simplified by the provision of a gape, a wide soft aperture, a mouth, into which the parent can easily place food. In the course of growing, this gape narrows, and hardens, and the maturing beak slowly develops to its final type. However, the chicks of ground nesting birds do not have these wide, soft gapes. Their beaks are already formed for use to the pattern of maturity, though they have still to harden and develop.

Some species, the Herring gull is one, have a red spot on the lower mandible. This is thought to be of assistance when feeding, a guide to the young to the food source. It raises the question of the colour sense in birds. Undoubtedly, they can distinguish dark and light shades in the same way perhaps as bees do, but there seems to be no grounds for assuming that a colour sense, as we know it, is there. Why the red spot is in some species and not others is obscure.

Instances of attempts of parents to teach their young to fly have been reported. It is unwise to place too much human interpretation on the actions of wild creatures, but birds give us opportunities for close contacts and intimate association with them, and we are impressed by much in their lives that corresponds with our own, arising from the same feelings and motives, as far as can be judged.

Snowy owl and young ones.

Above: *A puffin colony at Lundy.* Below: *Young song thrushes awaiting food from parents.*

Above: *An example of the bird table described on page 65.* **Below:** *A remarkable demonstration of natural camouflage; these 16-day-old Nightjars sleep out in the open on heathland, depending on their disruptive colouring for protection. (Douglas F. Lawson).*

With all fledgelings, the most dangerous time for them is the period immediately after leaving the nest, emerging into the world for the first time. They are defenceless, and must rely on camouflage, and cover for security, plus the priceless instinct of remaing still when danger threatens. Of course, they are under surveillance of their parents, and many instances are on record of the courage which the adult birds show in defending their young, bluffing, feigning injury and displaying hostility to good purpose. It is clear that during times of danger they are able to convey to the young by calls and other actions how best to act until the danger has passed.

As with bird identification itself, the keen bird watcher can make up a nesting log, an example of which is given here. Again a note-book suffices and the same book can be used year after year for comparative purposes. Naturally you may not have an opportunity for observing many nests, but country dwellers should certainly find such a project feasible.

NESTS: Species	Where Seen	Date	Number of eggs	Young hatched	Fledged	Remarks

CHAPTER SEVEN

THE AMAZING FLYING MACHINE

THE WHOLE BODY of a bird is designed primarily to give it efficiency in the air: its organs, internal, and external structures such as feathers and wings, its hearing and eyesight. These physical attributes are augmented by quick emotional reactions to obstacles, disturbances such as air currents, and winds, and exceptional alertness, quick movements and vitality.

Here then is an amazing flying machine.

SIGHT

Overall, the eyesight of a bird is vastly superior to ours. Unlike humans, most species lack frontal vision except when turning their head sideways, but it is no handicap as heads can be moved with great facility. Moreover, the eyes, except in a few species, being in the side of the head give the widest possible radius of vision. Each eye works independently of the other. They are large for the size of the bird. In fact, birds may be said to have binocular sight, and some them stereoscopic sight.

The pupils ensure a sharp focus on distant objects, and are not sensitive to blue light rays, like ours, which reflect hazy conditions. It seems that red attracts birds, being the most conspicuous colour in their vision, and it is interesting to note that many of the berries or fruits, on which they feed, and rely upon for sustenance in winter are crimson or red.

The excellent sight of birds applies to all the species, irrespective of size, and reaches a level of efficiency to meet the demands of their daily lives. As might be expected, therefore, the birds of prey, as a group, have the best vision, the hawks, falcons, owls.

Carrion-eating birds like the vultures sense the carcasses of dead animals from afar. It may be that they have not seen the food but take their cue from the movement of other vultures nearer to the carcass, which they can see from a great height and distance. Again, that familiar hawk, the Kestrel, can be seen hovering in the air, and this slowing down, and remaining almost stationary in

The Stormy petrel remains at sea except when breeding or when driven ashore by very bad weather. It is well known for its skimming gliding flight over the wave tops, its feet sometimes trailing in the water. Only about 6½ inches long, it is the smallest bird in Britain with webbed feet.

flight, enables its eyes to pick up the movements of small creatures below on which it feeds.

The eyes of the owls have special features. Their large, rounded heads accommodate both eyes in front and they have frontal vision like us. The conical facial discs with which their eyes are surrounded gather all the light available. This is especially necessary for their activities at night, when out of doors there is rarely total darkness because of light from the stars, even from far distant ones which we cannot see.

Water birds can see straight ahead and sideways, and are thus able to pick up objects near to them in the suffused light beneath the water surface.

HEARING

With a few exceptions such as some owls, birds do not have visible ears, but this lack of a conspicuous external ear, such as that in humans and mammals, does not impair their hearing. On the contrary, their hearing is very acute.

Some species have small external ears which are not seen unless the feathers surrounding them are parted; Others do not have external ears but internal auditory organs which are placed behind the eye.

Birds can hear sounds outside the range of human hearing. Most bird utterances are fairly high pitched compared with the more gutteral noises made by such species as the rook, crow, heron, even the cuckoo, and sea birds. Owls with their large microphonic ears can hear the rustling of small mammals on the ground. Their soft plumage which ensures silent flight allows other sounds to be more audible at night. Here again the agility with which birds can move their heads and bodies, aids their hearing – and this is used to good purpose. Most of us will have seen a Song thrush on the lawn with its head slightly sideways, apparently listening to a worm, or worms, moving in the soil.

Birds are highly selective in their hearing, meaning that they recognise instantly the calls and songs not only of their own species but of others, cries indicative of anxiety, anger, fear, pain and pleasure; and the noises which have meaning for them are picked out, showing a high degree of selectivity from the mixed sounds which do not strictly form part of their world. Even the shattering noise of low flying aircraft and trains is largely ignored as being of no concern to them, though it is noticeable that staccato noises, bangs, cracks, and reports disturb them when their defensive or protective mechanism reacts instantly to such alarms. However, birds get used to noises which they hear regularly, or occasionally, in their habitats, accepting them as an ingredient of the terrain.

SMELL

In one respect birds are deficient if we compare them with humans and mammals. They have little sense of smell, and most species do not seem to be able to smell at all. This is not necessary for them as for us, or four-footed creatures. The latter definitely use smell for direction finding, and some, as in the case of dogs, interpret a kind of smell language. They make their mark as they proceed, and pick up the scent again on a return journey. Also, they recognise when others of the same, or kindred species, have passed that way.

All this in the case of birds is not required. In the air, even if they could emit smells these would be quickly dispersed by the winds and air currents; and for direction they rely on a special sense, or mechanism. The more or less lack of smell in birds is therefore an interesting example of nature confining the attributes for life in any species strictly to what is necessary, a simplification that is very important.

Birds, therefore, do not react to offensive smells. Eagles, hawks, and other birds of prey leave the discarded parts of carcasses, bones, fur, etc, adjacent to their nests. There is no attempt at cleanliness in this respect. Apparently the distasteful odour is not offensive to them, or to their young and is not harmful to them.

But vapours and fumes are registered and evaded, as is pollution of the atmosphere, which might cause discomfort, being signalled by their sense organs, which are not conspicuous. These small apertures are near to the base of the beak, used for breathing, and lead to cavities that react to smells sufficient to add to the birds' sense of taste. In this, as with us, though less marked, it seems that taste and smell sense are to some extent complementary in birds.

As regards taste, a simple indication is the preference of some birds, blackbirds are an example, for sweet instead of cooking apples, only to be expected, but interesting none the less. A lady asked me if she should throw out rotten apples, thinking that they might be harmful to birds. The answer is that they much like rotten apples, useful in winter when food is scarce, and enjoyed especially by blackbirds.

AWARENESS

With specially keen eyesight and hearing to which a reference has been made in preceding notes, birds seem to possess an overall sense of great importance to them. This is not something that can be explained with exactitude, but their excellent eyesight and hearing contribute to it. This sense of awareness of danger, or disturbance, the instant recognition of anything detrimental to them is a kind of protective cloak.

Rooks have been known to vacate their nesting trees after many years of habitation when to all appearances these were in good condition. In such cases, after a lapse of time, one or more of the

Whin-chat.   *Stone-chat.*

trees have fallen, and others have turned from their apparently sound state to one of slow decay. Did rooks know what was pending?

As the desertion of rooks of an old established rookery caused misgivings in many country places years ago, there must have been a build-up of evidence giving rise to fears so widely held.

Again, it was pointed out by Richard Jefferies that rooks in a field did not seem to mind a farmer with a stick, even when he carried it under his arm as one would a gun; but when he had a gun, or a rifle, they were careful to keep a safe distance from him.

During World War 2 there were a number of reports of pheasants and geese heralding a bombing raid by their persistent calling – the sense of something dangerous, or disturbing, approaching.

The same is observed in our smaller birds whose demeanour sometimes clearly indicate when something is wrong. The presence of a bird of prey is quickly sensed, and the alarm raised. It is interesting to note that the cuckoo, though not a predator, but a 'sponger' on several species of small birds who are obliged to act as foster parents to its young, often causes a commotion and is

Nightingale.

chased off. This could be because the cuckoo is something like a hawk in appearance. Despite this, cuckoos are successful in planting their eggs in nests because they watch and wait for an opportunity to do so.

From this we see that birds are highly selective and sensitive, with quick responses to anything unfavourable to their welfare. This high sense of awareness helps to safeguard their existence in the highly vulnerable environment in which they have to exist.

Except in the larger and stronger birds of prey, birds are not physically equipped for defence against enemies, thus they must rely on an 'early warning system', remain still, or take cover, and trust in their protective colouring, which in many species is remarkably effective, and changes with the seasons to help to disguise them in their habitats.

CALLS AND SONGS

Calls and songs make up the language of birds. To us calls seem to be more conversational than songs. They are uttered throughout the year whereas most songs are seasonal in their duration, heralding the courtship and the breeding period, and, in general, song is continued while these last.

Those species which habitually have three broods have a longer song period, as might be expected, seeing that song and young are so closely associated. The Yellow hammer, or Yellow bunting, is one, and so is the Wood pigeon, or Ring dove, with an extended breeding season producing a succession of 'Twins'. Of course, the *coo-oow-oow-cuk* of the Wood pigeon is its song, as is the call of the cuckoo its song. These may not be very melodious to us musically, but to the birds they are just as important as those of the finest songsters in our estimation, ie, the nightingale and the blackcap. These broken songs of the Wood pigeon and the Cuckoo perform the same service in the life cycle.

Calls express anxiety, aggression, and other intimations: they are used during the period of song and are supplementary; they are also used when there is no song. Calls form a communal or social language, not only amongst birds of the same species, but many of them are understood by other species, ie, denoting hostility. While both calls and song are instinctive, the young round off their 'speech' through repetition by the parents. There is also the interesting feature of bird mimicry, more pronounced in some species than in others, not only of the calls and songs of other birds, but of sounds about them with which they become familiar and can imitate, even the human voice. Of British wild birds the starling seems to be the most notable mimic.

In the song lives of birds, the dawn and evening choruses make the greatest impact upon us. These performances last at their peak for about twenty minutes or longer dependent on the weather conditions, and die away. Why do birds sing thus, to greet the new day before they feed themselves, or their young ones? It must be an all compelling urge. Are these songs of joy, or are there more practical reasons for the outbursts, a competitive spirit? Again, are they declaring their territories anew, and constantly, morning and evening, though this latter peak song period is not usually quite so full or so sustained as is the one in the morning?

It is not possible to answer these questions with certainty. It is likely that a number of considerations generate song activity, with the coming of the light and during its recession. We cannot read a bird's mind, but it is clear that they do not sing for us, but for some purpose of their own which is an integral part of their breeding ritual, perhaps it is all best explained by the old saying 'A bird sings because it must!'

As might be expected, the organs of a bird which enable it to produce calls and songs are very different from ours. Some of these calls and songs are too faint, or too high pitched, to be heard by us though, of course, they can be heard by other birds. Simply stated, the vocal mechanism of a bird consists of a syrinx, a two-pronged organ inside its chest through which the muscles force air, and this compressed air causes the fine membrane walls of the chest to vibrate and thus emit sounds, calls, and song music.

Often the call or song of a bird is the first sign of its presence. There are species which are difficult to identify from others, but when heard their songs leave no doubt, when the song is known to the listener. Years ago it took a long time to get familiar with so many varied calls and songs; now, excellent gramophone records are available, and played over in the home, it is easy, and pleasant, to get to know all the more common birds we are likely to hear.

Perhaps the nightingale and the blackbird are our best known singers, but here the Blackbird, Song thrush and Skylark deserve mention.

CALLS AND SONGS AT NIGHT

Some birds sing during the day and also at night being diurnal and nocturnal. They include the following:

> Nightingale
> Nightjar
> Sedge warbler
> Reed warbler
> Grasshopper warbler
> Blackcap
> Woodlark

The first two sing more at night than during the day, especially around dawn and before midnight. The Grasshopper warbler

Redstart.

possibly less so, and the others may be said to be largely daytime singers. Owls seem to be wholly nocturnal, though when mobbed by other birds, or otherwise disturbed in their roosts, they may demonstrate during daylight hours. The little owl flies and hunts by day.

FLIGHT

Flight consists of movements and evolutions which are hereditary, or instinctive, in a species. It takes the form of a distinct pattern by which we can identify birds by their flight, once we have become familiar with it.

Some birds fly long distances, others make short flights, some cruise along, and there are those that dive earthwards, or into the water; some soar, glide and hover. Thus the pattern is one of great variety and fascination, and includes the undulating flight of woodpeckers, tits, and other small birds.

To enable birds to fly and move in the air efficiently the whole of the body, and the wings and tail are shaped to this end. The front edge of the wing is firm and inflexible, but the rear of the wing gives and yields to pressures. Thus the front gives penetrating force, as it were, while the rear edge is used for balancing and braking.

Generally, it is the large-winged birds that soar, such as the albatross, osprey, kite, and others. This is because their wings provide a surface large enough for rising air currents to take effect. Power for flight is derived from the comparatively large and strong muscles that lie forward to the front of the breast, and from these the wings obtain their driving force.

The mechanics of flight can be scientifically interpreted – the balance of the body and air penetration, the commencement of the flight from the ground or sea level, the gathering of power to rise, and the braking action for descent when the tail is brought into play. All the components of the body finely synchronise to make a bird's flight perfect.

The dive of the gannet is spectacular with the large bird making a streamlined entry into the water, wings folded, its whole body, beak and legs, in a line helped by its substantial weight to make a power-dive on the fish below. Gannets know the presence and movements of shoals of fish, and dive into them sure of a catch. The height from which they begin their dive seems to be related to the depth at which the fish are swimming below the surface.

In contrast to the gannet, the Little tern makes quick, repeated descents to the water for fish from a low height, taking them from near the surface, and in doing so often the bird splashes on to the water as it extracts its prey.

The undulating, or dipping form of flight previously mentioned is best seen in the woodpecker, the wagtail, and to some extent the chaffinch and the tits. They make short, cruising flights, the resistance at the front of the wings being greater than in those of the larger birds. This causes them to fly at less speed, and in a more confined area, to check their flight, descend, or alight, with greater facility.

The wing of a bird is essentially a forearm specially developed to facilitate flight. The three types of feather, long, medium, and short are known as primary, secondary and tertiary, in biological terms.

The Skylark is a bird which has strongly developed wings for its specialised kind of hovering flight.

The tiny goldcrest often assumes a posture something like that of a humming bird when a rapid vibration of the wings enables it to hover, or flutter, in front of foliage without touching it.

Perhaps the peregrine gives the best display of a swift, dashing flight, low over obstacles in pursuit of small hedgerow birds. Mention should be made of the semi-hovering, zigzagging flight of the snipe, both the Common and Jack species, which is part of their courtship display, being accompanied by a distinct humming, or droning (perhaps a buzzing best describes it) caused by the vibrations of the tail feathers and their impact upon the air.

THE WEIGHT OF BIRDS

Appearances are deceptive, and birds which largely exist in the air are remarkably light in weight for their size. Species that spend most of their time on land, though using the air at will, and for passage, are generally of a heavier type, for instance, ducks. Those on the wing most of the time, such as the two *hirundines,* the swallow and house martin, and the swift, are extremely buoyant and light in weight to enable them to operate effectively in an aerial environment.

The special attributes that contribute to lightness in birds are their bones, which are aerated, or hollow, very different from the solid bones of mammals, The feathers are the lightest covering possible for the body, a horny and flexible rib running down the centre from which the sprigs of feathers grow, graduated in size and overlapping, thus forming air sacs, and a soft, warm, and strong outer covering.

Finches and such small birds weigh little more than a half-ounce, the Tree-creeper and the tiny Goldcrest considerably less, the Song thrush about one and three-quarter ounces, the Swift just over an ounce, and the Swallow barely exceeds half-an-ounce. The Common heron looks to be a large bird, with its long legs and neck, but may weigh from 15 to 18 pounds, the Gannet about 7 pounds, roughly 3 pounds less than the Golden eagle; a cormorant may weigh 7 pounds and geese from 5 to 9 pounds.

Weight, of course, varies at different times of the year, with the food supply, and most birds tend to weigh heaviest in the autumn when they are building up a reserve of fat. In particular, the migrating species put on weight by as much as a third or a quarter to create a reserve of fat as fuel for the migratory passage.

It is the feathers that make birds look heavier than they are; for instance, the owls always appear to be plump, and well fed, and fairly heavy birds: but a Barn owl is unlikely to weigh more than 8-10 ounces, and a Little owl 6-7 ounces.

The front of a bird is the lightest part of its body. The head, or cranium, is covered by only a thin mesh of bone. Lack of teeth also contribute to lightness; The horny rims of the beak which to some extent take their place, are a lighter embellishment. The most weighty organs are near the centre of gravity, and the strongest muscles, for obvious reasons, are in the wings and the legs; but the weight of the heart of a bird is higher than in most mammals compared to the weight of its body. This provides the rapid heart beats necessary to feed the circulatory system furnishing vitality, strength and warmth.

BIRDS AND THE WEATHER

Birds being creatures of the air are more subject to weather influences than grounded mammals, especially winds and air currents. As we have seen, they are bodily equipped to live and flourish in their aerial environment.

As we know, winter is often a severe time for them. Extensive periods of hard frost bring the worst conditions, with cold winds freezing the water and making the ground iron hard. Obviously water birds are liable to suffer in these conditions as are birds such as woodpeckers, wrens, tits, and even the familiar blackbirds and thrushes, though many garden birds are saved in a bad spell by the food and water put out for them by householders.

Such is the biological make-up of a bird's body, its metabolism, that it is able to function so as to provide the body temperature necessary to withstand reasonably cold weather. Actually, few birds perish from the cold. It is lack of food in hard conditions, with gradually diminishing strength, that is fatal to so many. They simply fade away.

Those winter visitors, the redwings, though coming to Britain from Northern Europe, are very susceptible to British severe weather, and many of them perish. This again is largely due to lack of food. Berries, of which they take more at the end of winter, are eaten until few remain to feed the hungry flocks. That other winter visitor, the fieldfare, also from Northern Europe, a larger and stronger bird than the redwing, is able to withstand severe weather better.

Where do birds find shelter during the long, cold winter nights? How are they able to endure the cold? These are questions which are constantly asked.

Grey Plover. (Robin Williams).

One of the finest examples of nest construction is that of the reed warbler; position and depth are well shown in this photograph by Ernest Mytum, of a pair attending their young, one with an eye on the camera.

The answer to the first is that many water birds remain on their waters in reservoirs, lakes, and ponds, and can manage as long as the water does not get iced up. Many gulls float out the night on the water of their accustomed roosting places, but probably more stand packed together on the adjacent land. The birds in the centre obviously get some shelter from those surrounding them, and the tendency is noticeable for late birds coming to roost to try and settle in the mass of gulls which have already taken up their positions.

Tree and hedgerow birds find shelter in evergreens, yew, holly ivy, and the densest cover available, bramble thickets, woods, and plantations. Some prefer buildings, and hollows, or holes, in trees.

As weather obviously is a powerful influence on birds and their movements, it is to be expected that they have a keen awareness of its changes, of the rise and fall in temperature which a change brings. The approach of thunderstorms seems to be recognised by some species more than others, notably the pheasant, as indeed by cattle and horses which cavort about the fields in warm, sultry weather.

Swifts, swallows, and House martins fly higher in the sky in settled weather because the insect life on which they feed ascends higher. Rooks forage for food further away from their nesting, or roosting trees, whereas when storms or unsettled weather is about, they tend to do the day's foraging nearer their base. In this respect, the behaviour of rooks is held to be a reliable indication of the weather by observant country people. Also, when they build their nests in spring high up in the tops of trees it is held to be a reliable sign that the summer will be a good one.

Birds take advantage of thermal currents to glide and soar, and evolution has made them masters of this art to enable them to make the best use of their aerial environment to conserve their energy.

Migratory birds take advantage of favourable winds to assist their passage. Generally, birds avoid flying head in to wind, if it is at all strong, for the simple reason that it opposes their progress and uses up energy. Birds always stand facing the wind (notice gulls on recreation grounds), as this avoids ruffling their feathers, and is thus more comfortable for them.

The feather layers of birds provide them with effective bodily covering. The different textures – soft down feathers, the harder and firmer exterior ones, overlapping afford a specially good overcoat, as it were. Further, as the heart beats of a bird are rapid, more so in cold weather, they can generate extra bodily heat. Also it is noticeable how birds puff out their feathers when it is very cold; this aids circulation and makes their protective covering more effective.

Thus, given sufficient food, the bodily make-up of a bird ensures survival, and for a considerable time even if its food is at starvation level. However, sometimes there is unusually severe wintery weather, with arctic conditions for several weeks, a notable example being the winter of 1962-63. Many species suffered severely, and the reduction in numbers of wrens, woodpeckers, and others was noted in following years. Water birds, including swans, were found frozen in the ice, and even small areas of ice free water became difficult to find. These conditions also led to unexpected birds turning up in unusual places.

As might be assumed, the weather influences the feeding pattern of birds. In a high wind they are obliged to seek food where they can in the more sheltered places, and in these conditions species such as the chiff-chaff and goldcrest may be seen feeding on the ground, though normally they do so in bushes and trees.

Above: *The Scaup. (Douglas F. Lawson).* **Below:** *A male Kingfisher with his prey.*

Gertie, an oiled guillemot, cleaned, nursed for several weeks, taught to swim again, and released into the sea by K. James. (J. W. Kitchenham Ltd.).

CHAPTER EIGHT

BIRDS IN THE GARDEN

I F A F E W S I M P L E facilities are provided birds can be attracted to a garden and induced to become residents, indeed House sparrows, tits, greenfinches, starlings, blackbirds, and Song thrushes require little inducement: others such as the Hedge sparrow, wren, and these days the chaffinch are missing from many gardens in which they were once seen in suburban and built-up areas around our towns. They are still, of course, a part of most country gardens.

Food, water, suitable cover, and nesting boxes are the prime requirements. Keen gardeners can still cultivate their plots according to taste while accommodating the birds. These may be considered complementary to any garden, making it more pleasant and interesting with their songs, colours, and movements. Some will say 'Yes, but what about the damage they do?' Much of the harm which they seem to be doing is not real but liable to be exaggerated unless we look into the matter carefully. One thing is clear, it is a poor garden without any birds and better described as an 'out-door greenhouse'. Over a year, season by season, birds pay for their keep in more ways than one.

As to food, in addition to household scraps – fats, cheese, broken wholemeal biscuits, and mixed seed which may be put out for them – they can be provided with as much natural food as the size and character of the garden permits.

Sunflowers provide seed for finches. A rowan, or mountain ash tree is also decorative and its berries are well liked by blackbirds, starlings, and others; the elderberry, too, though perhaps not quite as acceptable to some gardeners. All the same, it is equally decorative with its large clusters of cream-coloured flowers, and the purple berries are taken eagerly by birds. Both rowan and elderberry can be pruned to taste and will still flower and fruit.

A home-made bird table, with suitable gadgets to hold particular kinds of food for different species of birds, not only has the merit of being far less expensive than bought articles but has the added advantages of being far more efficient for the job (since it can be made in the light of personal practical experience) and of providing a pleasant occupation for a few hours of one's spare time.

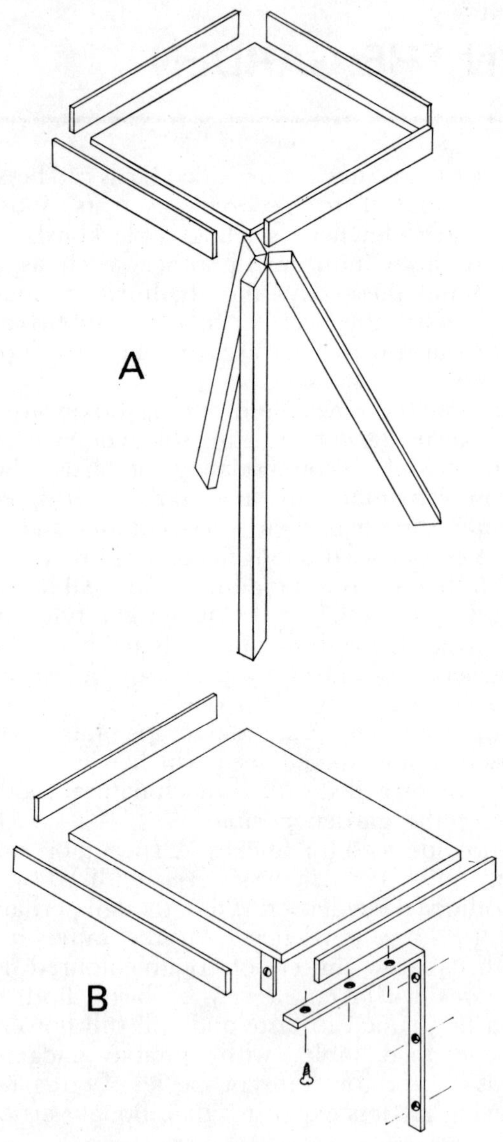

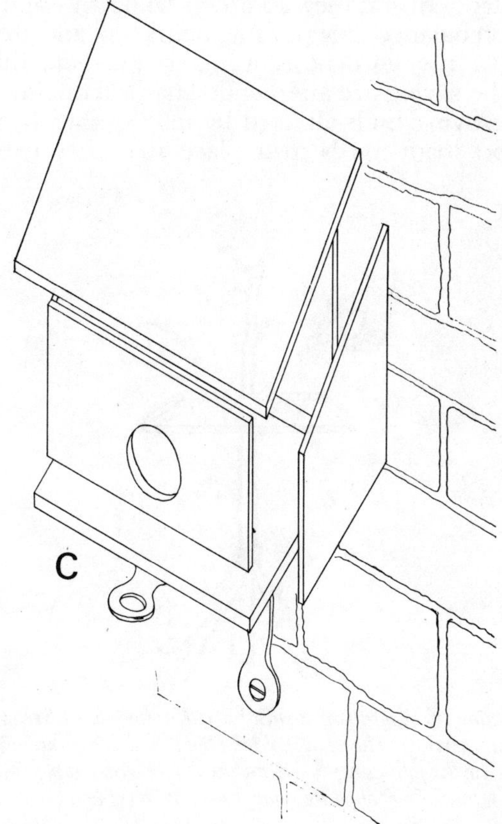

Three simple structures for attracting birds into the garden, with assembly given in 'exploded' form to show mode of construction. (A) Bird table. (B) Bird feeding tray for walls or outside windows in apartment blocks. (C) A form of nesting box for wall attachment by means of metal brackets. Dimensions are not critical (Kenneth M. Jones).

If a garden is large enough to permit a small wild patch to be allowed to remain undisturbed so much the better. A few weeds, groundsel, chicory, thistle, cow parsley, and teasel make a mixed bird menu when they seed. Bullfinches like the seeds of candytuft. The reputation of these handsome birds for destroying buds makes some gardeners disinclined to encourage them, but it is nice to have a pair around, and they do little real harm – and some good. Here again on balance they pay for their keep, and are as much an adornment to the garden as a plant. Further, their pruning activities in the spring are an intended natural operation, thinning out and destroying buds affected by insect pests. It is only when there are too many birds in a place that they cause any real damage.

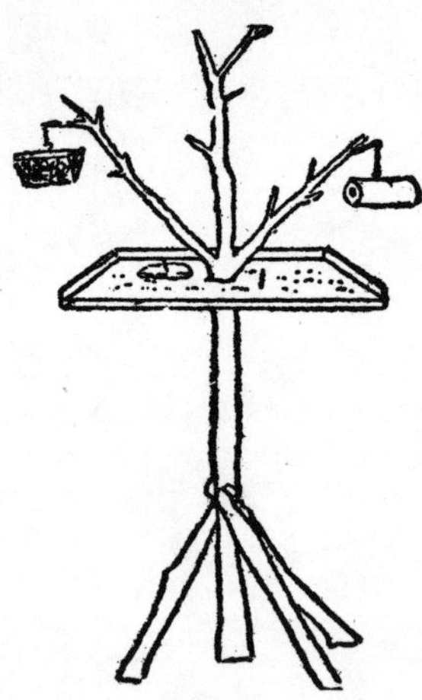

Here is a bird table incorporating a suitable cut-down small tree or sapling which provides natural perches. The seed holder (left) and the food holder (right) are shown in detail in the following two drawings. The seed hopper shown in the final drawing opposite may be stood on the table.

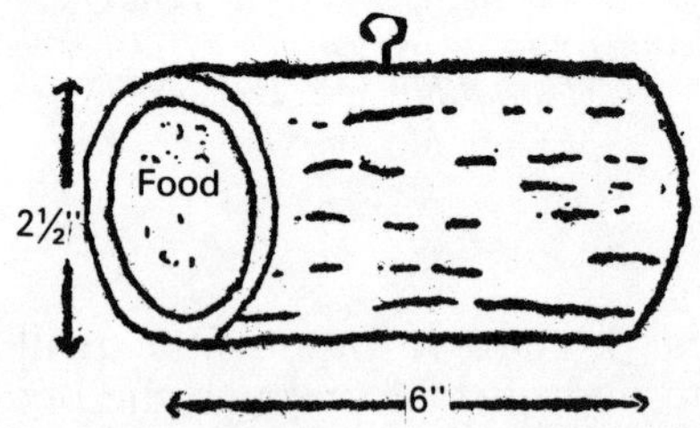

A small natural log looks best, but must be hollowed out as much as possible, so as to present the largest area of food to the birds. The log should be hung from a twig by a short length of picture wire terminating in a loop.

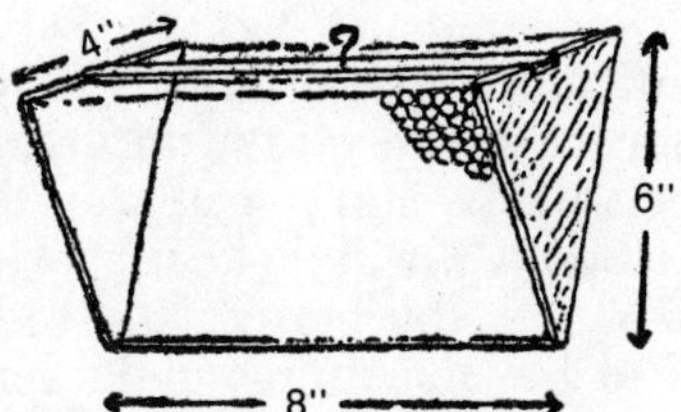

A small slat (8" by 1") across the top
keeps the whole rigid and provides a
base for the screw. ½" mesh netting, all
in one piece, stapled to wood triangles.
A rod (curtain rod) across the bottom
keeps the base rigid.

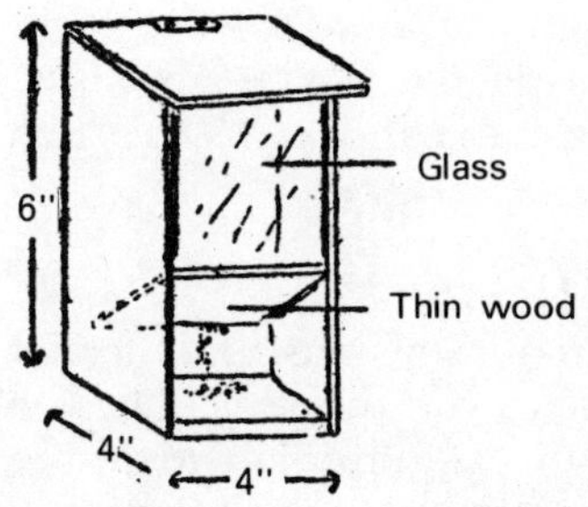

The lid of the hopper is hinged, for
filling, and projects a little in front.
The glass is held between tiny battens.
So is the sloping wood, which must not
quite touch the back, so that the seed can
trickle down to the tray at the bottom. A
slight rim should be provided in front
of the tray. If the hopper is hung up, the
base should project a little (say half an
inch) to provide perching ground.

Drawings are not to scale but suggested dimensions are given which make
structures suitable for garden birds.

Evergreens are important to birds. Holly, yew, and ivy offer their fruits, and are also valuable for the cover which they provide in winter! Laurel bushes, privet, and box are similarly liked by birds.

Too much tidying up of a garden destroys its attraction for birds: too much spraying can be harmful to them. With a little spare time available window and portable bird feeders, tables, and nest boxes can be made easily and cheaply. The plainer and more natural looking these are the better, and old wood is excellent. They do not need to be smartly painted. A simple tray, with an inch high border, or rim mounted on three supports makes an excellent feeder. Something similar, a window tray, fixed to the sill by two brackets is convenient for flats and maisonettes.

Nest boxes should be in position well before the nesting season, that is early in the year as birds look around for suitable sites some time before they are ready to begin building. Nest boxes should be fixed in sheltered positions, where there is not too much sun, or shade, and so placed that the cold north-easterly winds do not blow directly into them.

Cats are a menace, and it follows that all feeding places, and nest boxes must be out of their reach. When feeding birds on the ground do so in the open, clear of borders and other cover in which a cat might conceal itself, and wait, ready to pounce.

Of course water must be available throughout the year as birds like to bathe in winter as well as during the warmer months. A shallow dish, or tray, in which they can stand and splash themselves is preferred.

RINGING BIRDS

Questions arise concerning the birds in our gardens, and those that come to us from afar, from countries over the seas. These are answered to some extent when we can recognise individual birds. Is it the same blackbird, thrush, or robin that we see year after year? How long do they live? Is it the same swallow or House martin that arrives back each spring to its nesting site in a porch, or outhouse or under the eaves of the house; the same swifts returning to the same locality, the Yellow wagtails and the Sedge warblers by the river?

Each bird is an individual, with an expression and character of its own, but this is not obvious to us, and it is only when we can recognise a bird as an individual that it is possible to know with certainty its movements, its age, and other interesting features in its life cycle.

Young Thrush not yet able to fly. (Raymond Lea).

Above: Nightjar. (C. Sanderson Dolley). Below: The Spotted flycatcher is a summer migrant which can be seen in gardens, parks, orchards, and similar locations.

Occasionally a bird has a distinct colour marking, an irregularity in its plumage due to faulty pigmentation, or a blemish, an injured foot, or wing. An obvious example is the blackbird, a species subject to albinism, that is white colouration ranging from a single spot, or a feather, to an almost white bird. We can recognise it instantly, and because of this we take more interest in it.

Ringing was devised using Heligoland traps and mis-nets, with the purpose of keeping track, as it were, on individual birds. Ringing is now done on a world-wide scale, by accredited ringers, using rings bearing official cyphers, letters and numbers, indicating the country of origin. When and where ringed, examined and released, the time of the year, the weight of the bird, these, and other details, are entered in a ringing station's log book. Information is exchanged by the international network of centres which enables a bird to be reported upon and identified by its ring; much information regarding its movements thus becomes known.

It follows that only a very small percentage of the large number of birds ringed are traced, some are trapped, released, and re-trapped at the same place year after year; but the occasional one, with its tell-tale ring, can reveal new information about a species, and contribute to ornithological history.

For a serious study of birds, ringing is thus a valuable practice, and they do not seem to suffer undue physical harm when the operation is performed by competent operators. However, birds may suffer shock as a result of being caught and handled. It is now an offence under the Wild Birds Act to ring birds without a licence.

British rings are issued by the British Museum (Natural History), Cromwell Road, London SW1, in co-operation with the British Trust for Ornithology, Beech Grove, Tring, Herts., the controlling centre for ringing in Britain.

SONG INDICATORS

The Great Tit has a variety of notes. Some are rather guttural, or scratchy, and they may include a little from the vocabulary of other tits. The Great Tit sings or calls from a perching position, not in flight. One note is a 'pink' something like that of a chaffinch.

The main song may be heard from January to mid-May. This is loud and clear. It has been described as 'ringing his bell', or like the pumping up of a bicycle tyre, or 'teacher, teacher.'

The calls of **the Blue Tit** are ringing, harsh and disjointed, scolding – a 'tsee-tsee-tssit', most likely heard from February to mid-May.

The Coal Tit has a pleasant little repetitive song – a high pitched, thin 'tsee-tsee', twice, then a pause, and repeated as it moves about, possibly in a yew or other coniferous tree. The song is suggestive of that of the Goldcrest but slightly stronger. 'Weecho-weecho' is another interpretation. It can be heard from mid-February to May mostly, but in December and January when the weather is mild.

The Long-tailed Tit. 'Si si-si', soft conversational notes as the birds move about in family parties, and other notes 'tsirrup' and 'tupp'.

The Marsh Tit. The song can be described as 'schip-schip-schip', and some times 'schuppi-schuppi'. But there is a scolding note 'tchay', preceded by a 'pitchuu'.

The Willow Tit has a more musical song than the other tits, including a series of warbler-like notes, interspersed with high pitched squeaky notes, and a plaintive 'piu-piu'.

The Bearded Tit's song is a simple 'ping-ping', or 'ching-ching' – a twang.

The Crested Tit. This truly Scottish species has a contact note 'si-si-si', sometimes preceeded with a short trill.

The Goldcrest's song is thin, and faint, lasting several seconds, and though it cannot be heard more than a few yards off, it is a useful indicator of the bird's presence, in a yew, pine or other coniferous tree. It begins haltingly, gathers pace into a 'ee-zeer-ee-zeer' run on, lasting several seconds, with a slight rise and fall, ending abruptly. It may be heard in any month, but mainly during March, April and May.

The Spotted Flycatcher is thought to be the most silent bird on the British list. (Gilbert White). Its scarcely audible song has to be listened for, in still conditions, a little medley of short, not unmusical notes, something like those of the House-martin, and also suggestive of bits of the linnet's song.

The Pied Flycatcher has a more pronounced song than the Spotted Flycatcher, a pleasant 'tzit-tzit--trui-trui-trui-' uttered rapidly, almost trill-like.

The Blackcap. Gilbert White described it as a wild song, very apt. It sings with abandon, a joyous, sweet melody, mellow with notes suggestive of the Nightingale, though not so halting. Sometimes there are seconds pauses between each but during the peak period of song, a long, running sequence.

The Garden Warbler is noted for the long, even duration of its song. It goes on and on, a surprising continuous song, mellow, fluent, with no unevenness, a delightful series of warbles.

The Wood Warbler, or **Wood Wren** keeps very much in the trees, and sings from mid-April to mid-May, halting notes gathering speed until they fuse into rapid shivering song. It sings on the wing, and sometimes rising and parachuting down, pipit-like.

The Willow Warbler. Best described as a silvery song, which rises and falls away into a whisper, to be repeated.

The Chiff-chaff – a chirrupper (Gilbert White) repeats 'chiff-chaff' continually. Sings in spring and on its autumn homeward passage.

The Common Whitethroat – a staccato song, scratchy and broken, but also warbling. Sings from a perch as well as rising above its song position.

The Lesser Whitethroat is a shy bird, heard before it is seen – a strong, pleasant warble, worked up from halting, quavering notes, into a long running passage.

The Chaffinch. His song is noteworthy for its consistency of pattern, and repetition over the greater part of the day during the peak singing time, from about mid-February to late May or early June. The rate of delivery is roughly seven or eight times to the minute. In a long spring day the output of song is impressive – a truly energetic performance. The bird has a sub-song or call 'pink', 'pink', and it is known by this name in some localities.

When it begins to sing it is only capable of producing the first part of the song sentence. It may take a week or ten days, seemingly to depend on the temperature, before the full sentence is completed.

The Greenfinch. Its song is best described as canary-like, a series of short, halting trills, gathering speed, and repeated until it works up into an unexpected 'wheeze', or 'zeeaire', followed again by trills and tinkles, sometimes in flight.

The Linnet. Its song may be heard in any month but April to early June is the peak period for it. It is variable with twittering notes, and trills, with phrases of two or three notes very pure in tone, and it sings in flight as well as when perching.

The Bullfinch utters a piping call, hardly a song, which is apt to vary from being scarcely audible to a clear, flute-like even call, and it also has a low inward sub-song.

The Dunnock or **Hedge-sparrow.** In mild weather it can be heard in December, and more so, of course, as spring approaches. The song is best described as a 'cheerful warbling.' It is a 'tweetle, tweet-le, tweet-le', six or seven of these to the minute. Often one bird is answered by a cock in an adjacent territory, and a pleasant duet continues, each bird waiting for the other to finish his 'tweetling' before taking it up himself. This can be heard early in the year in bright, frosty weather, with a rise in temperature.

The Wren. For a small bird, the Wren has a very strong song, a burst, or an explosion, which can be heard over a considerable distance. W. H. Hudson described it as 'a loud, bright, lyric'. It sometimes begins with a broken note or two then bursts into the ecstatic ripple, and ends abruptly.

The Woodpigeon or **Ring-Dove.** Its song is a simple 'coo-coo-coo-coo' repeated, occasionally with a separate 'coo' at the commencement, and always with a final separate 'coo' which ends abruptly. I have heard it described quite well by the sentence 'You fool, you poor fool, you.' There is also a sub-song, and a low pleasant murmur of the cock to the hen during the breeding season. It has a gliding courtship flight, and claps its wings over the back.

The Collared Dove has a low murmuring 'coo-coo' during the breeding season when its main call is a triple 'coo-coo-cuk', the final 'cuk' on a higher note and ending abruptly.

The Turtle Dove. This summer visitor can be heard from early May. A pleasant distinctive purring, basically a series of soft 'coos' merged into a level 'purr,' 'purr'. It also has a gliding courtship flight.

The Green Woodpecker or **'Yaffle'** has a call very much like 'yaffle', 'yafflle', loud and clear which can be heard over a considerable distance. The Green Woodpecker seldom drums. It has a short repeated 'pee', 'pee' cry. It can be heard in any month mainly from January to June, and in the autumn.

The Greater-Spotted Woodpecker or **'Pied'** is noted for its loud drumming, which can be heard early in the year, and more frequently as the breeding season proceeds. This curious noise can be heard up to half a mile or more away. It seems to be made by the bird striking the trunk, or large branch of a tree, rapidly with its beak, so rapidly that the movement is a blur which produces the continuous sequence of 'creaking', or drumming'. In this species the noise is a shorter burst, and louder than the Lesser-Spotted Woodpecker.

The Lesser-Spotted Woodpecker or **'Barred'**, the smaller of the two, drums similarly but in bursts of longer duration, and not as loud as the **Greater.**

The Nightjar. Another bird with a curious call, or song, a ripple of short, staccato notes which are emitted in an even flow of popping noises – a churring or jarring rattle; best heard from mid-May to July, it commences usually at sunset. Another characteristic sound is the clapping of its wings over the back.

The Wryneck. A summer visitor, now uncommon, makes a loud, clear 'pee' 'pee' call, not unlike that of the Kestrel – 'kek-kek-kek'.

The Mistle Thrush or **'Storm-cock'.** The loud, challenging song of this bird can be heard from mid-January onwards, but ceases at the end of April when most other birds are getting into their stride.

Usually it sings from the top-most branch of a tree, and the clear wavering notes are repeated in short phrases, time and again, shouted out, as it were, for all the world to hear. It is a mellow, rich song, with flute-like notes, though broken.

The Song Thrush, or **'Throstle'**, has a more varied and musical song than the **Mistle Thrush.** It often begins with a 'zeeter', 'zeeter', loud, long notes, followed by variations of flute-like notes, and repetitions, halting and clear.

Snatches of song may be heard in November, December and January, but it is about mid-February that the full range is heard, and often quite late as dusk is falling.

The Blackbird has claims to be our best singer, and though there are variations in individual birds, the mellow, even flow of notes, strung into short and longer phrases are unmistakable, noting also the effortless way in which the song is sustained. Usually, the blackbird sings from a perch, fully from mid-February until June or later, and occasionally a low warbling song is heard in the breeding season as the bird flies from one perch to another.

The Robin or **Redbreast** has two songs, basically the same, but clearly variant, an autumn and a spring song. The first comes after the moult in August – a plaintive, wistful, tender song, suiting the declining year, while the spring song is more vigorous, or spirited, and as with the song thrush is continued up to dusk.

The Robin has a sweet, inward warble, often sung by the cock perching close to his mate, obviously intended for her special benefit.

The full song consists of sweet, variable notes, built into phrases, never very long, without a pause, uttered quietly, without effort, and the impression is that the robin is singing to himself, for his own satisfaction, without a suggestion of a challenge or aggression.

The Nightingale has been more praised for its song than any other bird, but musically it is not as fine as that of the blackbird or robin. This is because the song consists of very broken utterances, stops and starts, notes churned out when suddenly the pure, rich flute-like notes emerge. Then the process of halting notes, and the build-up to the finest phrases begins again. The song period is short, from mid-April until early in June.

The Swift. Screaming parties of swifts are a familiar sight and sound in summer as they dash madly around their nesting sites, between houses, at great speed, some birds breaking away to fly up to the wall at the entrance to their nesting places.

This loud screeching, a 'sweeree-sweeree', loud and repeated, is really a wild exciting song of the species, though unmusical. It is full of meaning and expectancy, with eggs and young in the nests.

Swifts utter scratchy notes on the wing occasionally, and sometimes screech as they glide around, but it is only when in parties that the 'full song' is heard.

The Meadow Pipit sings in flight, the notes beginning as it rises, and they are repeated until the bird reaches the top of its ascent, which is not as high as that of the Tree pipit, when a succession of tinkling louder and more musical notes flow out, continued in the descent. It also sings from a perch, a post, or a stone wall, and is persistent in song during the breeding season.

The Tree Pipit, a summer visitor, is noted for a striking song display flight, and the song itself is pleasant and sustained. It consists of a series of canary-like notes, or sweet chirrups, gains momentum as the bird ascends and nears the peak of its rise when they become louder and more ecstatic. Then on stiff wings the bird parachutes down to a favourite perch, singing during the first part of its descent. It also sings from a perching station, the top of a tree, or low down on a bush near its nesting site.

The Reed Warbler. Its song is heard from the end of April throughout June, and snatches later, perhaps in August. It is monotonous, a series of jerky 'chirrups', irregular, not very musical, as it sings mostly out of sight in the swaying reeds. 'Tuc, tuc, tuc, whirr-whirr-whirr' – it goes on and on, with some mimicry.

The Sedge Warbler has a song which is basically the same pattern as that of the Reed, but harsher chirrupings, and more mimicry of the notes of other birds. There are musical notes as well as the predominate chattering. Sedge warblers will start to sing when they are disturbed at the nest, and when it is dark.

The Goldfinch. This bright bird has the most tinkling song of all the finches, sweet and melodious as it flits about on the seed heads of teasel, sow-thistle, groundsel and other plants, often in small parties. The snatches of song are short, with no harsh notes.

The Stonechat, a resident species, sings from mid-March to July. Its best song is a series of rapidly uttered double notes as the bird rises several feet into the air. Some are clear and sharp followed by others deeper in tone. There is a second type of song, uttered from a perching position, the top-most spray of gorse, or other bush, and this consists of scrappy, warbling noises, brief and jangled together.

The Whinchat, a summer visitor, usually seen in **Stonechat** country, has a brief song more musical than the latter, sweeter and clearer. It is heard from April to the end of June.

The Common Redstart is another summer visitor whose song is at its best during June. Its range of loud, rich and pure notes compel attention. They are warble-like and uttered in short phrases.

The Black Redstart can be heard in May and June. It consists of a burst of thin, scratchy notes followed by louder, warbling notes delivered four or five to the minute usually from the building on which it is likely to be nesting.

The Swallow. The song of the swallow is one of the sweetest summer sounds, very sweet and pure, with low, inward warbles, often when the cock is sitting by the side of his mate. Similar snatches of song are uttered on the wing and from perching positions.

The House martin. Its song is soft and musical but less subdued than that of the **Swallow**, with a simple inward warble, and sweet twitterings in flight as well as when perching.

The Sand martin. Less musical than those of the House martin, more hurried, and excitable, with quite a loud chorus among colonies at their nesting sites.

The Swift.

Above: 'Pigeon's milk' – a mealtime scene in the pigeon household. Below: The Long-eared owl is not common; it is fairly quiet and retiring. The 'ears' are actually tufts of feather. (Robert McCleod).

Above: *The watchful owlet quartet. They are of varied ages, the youngest at the left, the oldest peers over the young one's back at the camera. All were leg-ringed to check their movement after fledging. (John Warham).* **Below:** *These baby kestrels hatched on a transmission tower near Dungeness nuclear power station. After ringing (see opposite page) they were restored to their nest.*

Ringing a baby Kestrel before restoring it to its nest at a power station nesting site.

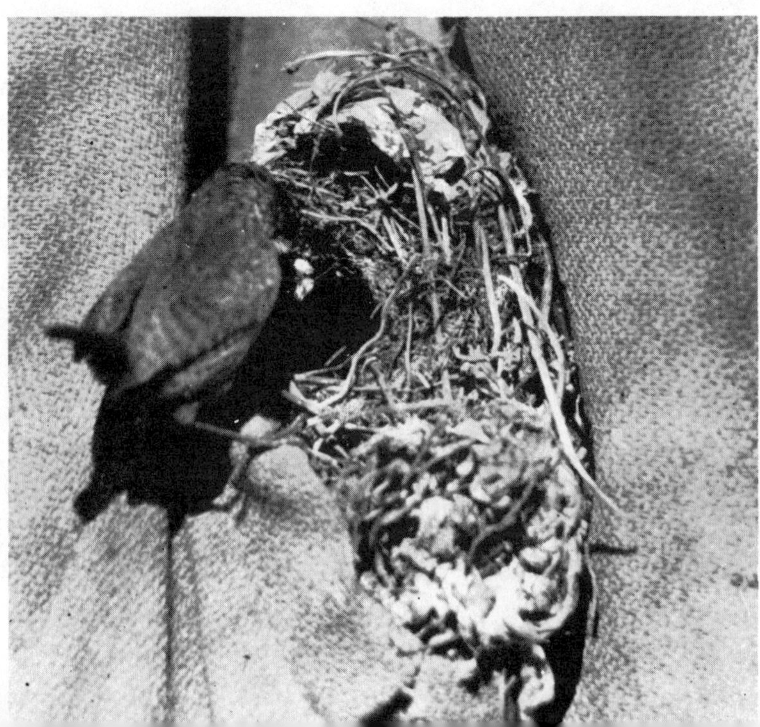

Above: *Members of the Surbiton and District Ornithological Society on a field study expedition.* **Below:** *A Wren just about to enter its nest which was built in the pocket of an old gardening coat left hanging in an outhouse. The Wren is noted for selecting unusual but convenient sites for its nest. (W. W. Pritchard).*

BIRD DISTRIBUTION

1: Species widely distributed in suitable habitats in England

Blackbird	Moorhen
Blue tit	Partridge
Bullfinch	Pied flycatcher (west and north)
Carrion crow	Pied wagtail
Chaffinch	Rook
Coal tit	Robin
Cuckoo	Reed bunting
Great Spotted woodpecker	Sand-martin
Great tit	Sedge warbler
Greenfinch	Skylark
Hedge sparrow	Song thrush
House-martin	Spotted flycatcher
House sparrow	Swallow
Jackdaw	Swift
Jay	Starling
Lapwing	Tawny owl
Little grebe	Tree creeper
Long-tailed tit	Whitethroat
Mallard	Willow warbler
Magpie	Woodpigeon
Mistle thrush	Wren
Mute swan	Yellowhammer

2: Species unlikely to be seen in Scotland

Avocet	Dartford warbler
Bearded tit	Firecrest
Bittern	Garganey
Black redstart	Grey phalarope
Black tern	Kentish plover
Bean goose	Hobby
Brent goose	Honey buzzard
Cirl bunting	Marsh harrier

Marsh warbler	Savi's warbler
Nightingale	Shore lark
Nuthatch	Spoonbill
Little-Ringed plover	Stone curlew
Lesser-Spotted woodpecker	Reed warbler
Red-necked Grebe	Teminick's stint
Red-legged partridge	Quail
Red kite	Woodlark

3: Species unlikely to be seen in Wales

Avocet	Little-Ringed plover
Bearded tit	Honey buzzard
Crested tit	Kentish plover
Barred warbler	Marsh harrier
Bean goose	Red-necked grebe
Bittern	Red-necked philarope
Capercallie	Rock dove
Dartford warbler	Savi's warbler
Dotterel	Shore lark
Great-Grey Shrike	Osprey
Golden eagle	Ptarmigan
Glaucous gull	Stone curlew
Firecrest	Velvet Scoter
Hobby	Waxwing
Iceland gull	Wryneck
Little auk	

4: Species not recorded in Ireland

Avocet	Great Spotted woodpecker
Barred warbler	Green woodpecker
Bearded tit	Lesser Spotted woodpecker
Bean goose	Hobby
Black grouse	Honey buzzard
Black-throated diver	Golden eagle
Capercallie	Goosander
Carrion crow (few)	Great Grey shrike
Crested tit	Hawfinch
Cirl bunting	Kentish plover
Dartford warbler	Lesser whitethroat
Dotterel	Little auk
Firecrest	Little gull

Little owl
Marsh warbler
Marsh tit
Nuthatch
Marsh harrier
Little-Ringed plover
Nightingale
Red kite
Red-legged partridge
Red-necked grebe
Red-backed shrike
Reed warbler

Ptarmigan
Savi's warbler
Smew
Osprey
Shore lark
Spoonbill
Stone curlew
Tawny owl
Teminick's stint
Willow warbler
Wood lark
Wood warbler

NB: A few of the species included in these lists are seen in the country under which they are shown, but, generally, are not expected to be sighted, and some of them have never been recorded.

SOME WATCHING PLACES

The venues listed below are either nature reserves or other areas designated specially for the preservation or study of bird life. In one or two instances (eg, Selborne) the area itself is listed as being of special interest though there is no actual bird watching facility. Locations which offer Field Study Centres (F.S.C.) or are under the auspices of the Royal Society for the Preservation of Birds (R.S.P.B.) are marked accordingly. Addresses of these two organisations are given at the end of the listing and they may be contacted (with a SAE) for further details.

Bradwell (Blackwater estuary), Essex.
Bardsey Island, Pembrokeshire.
Bass Rock, Firth of Forth, Scotland
Blakeney Point, Norfolk.
Bookham Common, Surrey.
Braunton Sands, Devon.
Brownsea Island, Hampshire.
Cemlyn Bird Observatory, Anglesey.
Church Norton, Sussex.
Cley, Norfolk.
Cuckmere Valley, Sussex
Dale Fort, Pembrokeshire (F.S.C.).
Dungeness, Kent (Bird Observatory).
Fair Isle, Shetland.
Farlington Marsh, Hampshire.
Farne Islands, Northumberland.
Flatford Mill, Suffolk (F.S.C.)
Grassholm, Pembrokeshire.
Havergate Island, Suffolk (R.S.P.B.).
Kingley Vale Nature Reserve, Sussex.
Langston Harbour, Hampshire.
Lundy Island, Devon.
May, Isle of Fife, Scotland.

Malham Tarn, Yorkshire (F.S.C.).
Minsmere, Suffolk (R.S.P.B.).
Monk's House, Northumberland (F.S.C.)
Newhaven Harbour, Sussex.
New Forest Hampshire.
Orielton, Pembrokeshire (F.S.C.).
Pagham Harbour, Sussex.
Peakirk Waterfowl Gardens, Northants (Wildfowl Trust).
Portland Bill Bird Observatory, Dorset.
Ramsey Island, Pembrokeshire.
Ravenglass, Cumberland.
Scolt Head, Norfolk.
Selborne, Hampshire (for associations with Gilbert White).
Stodmarsh, Nr. Canterbury, Kent.
St. Kilder, North Uist, Scotland.
Shetlands, Fair Isle, Feltar.
Skokholm Bird Observatory, Pembrokeshire.
Slapton Ley, Devon (F.S.C.).
Slimbridge, Gloucestershire (Wildfowl Trust).
Speyside, Inverness-shire, Scotland.
Spurn Head Observatory, Yorkshire.
Thorney Island, Hampshire.
Tring reservoirs, Hertfordshire.
Thursley Common, Surrey.

R.S.P.B. The Lodge, Sandy, Bedfordshire.
F.S.C.   Field Studies Council, Preston Mountford Hall,
         Mountford Bridge, Shrewsbury SY4 1DX.

THE LONDON AREA

In the royal parks an officially appointed Committee advises the Minister responsible on the maintenance of bird sanctuaries. This Committee has a network of accredited observers who record the birds seen, resident species, breeding species, and birds on passage. HMSO issues a yearly publication giving a list of the parks and the species recorded therein.

These parks are:

Bushey Park and Hampton Court Park
Greenwich Park
Osterley Park
Hyde Park and Kensington Gardens
Regent's Park and Primrose Hill
Richmond Park
Royal Botanical Gardens, Kew
St. James's and Green Parks

The whole of the London area, including a twenty mile radius from St. Paul's Cathedral, is carefully documented for its bird life by recorders for the London Natural History Society, and here again an annual report is published by the Society.

In and around London several large reservoirs are specially attractive to birds, and many species, including uncommon and rare ones are seen there from time to time, especially in the winter. These reservoirs are under the control of the London Water Authority, New River Head, Roseberry Avenue, London, EC4. Applicants for permits to visit the reservoirs must state their age, and if under 21, a sponsor is required.

More recreational facilities are being provided at some of the reservoirs as shown in the accompanying map.

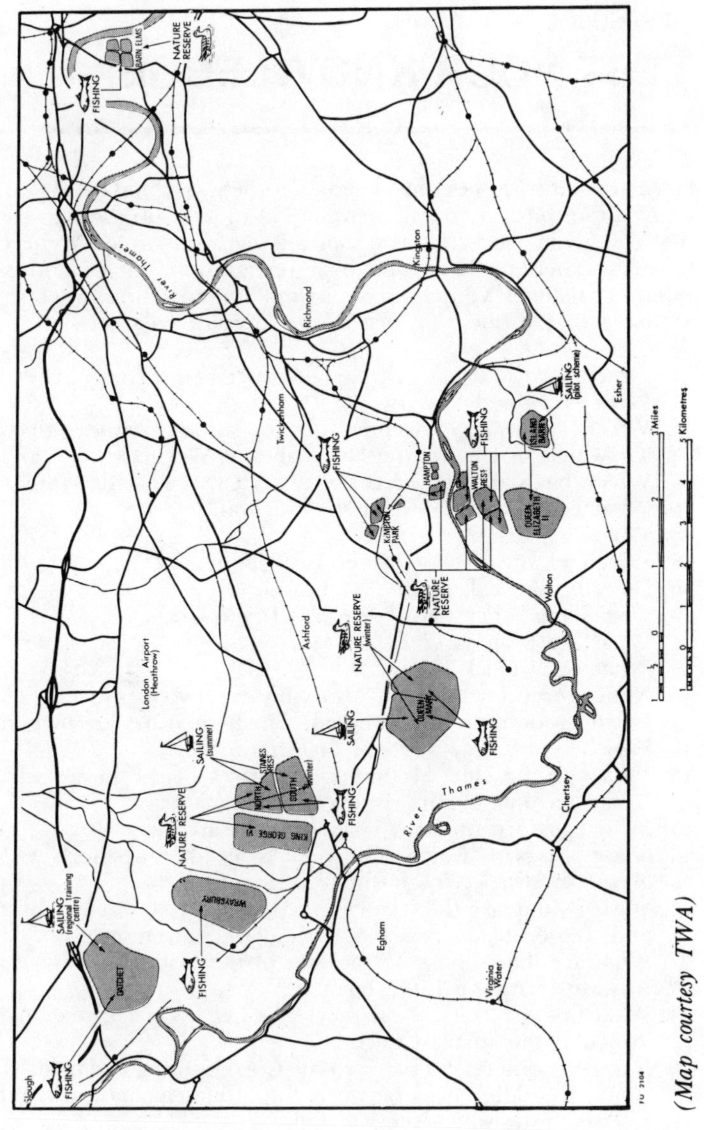

(Map courtesy TWA)

TEST YOUR KNOWLEDGE

Here are some 67 questions designed to help you find out how much you know about birds. Resist the temptation to look up the answers first and see how many questions you can answer right away. Write down the answers. Then consult your bird recognition books, and any other reference material you may have, to find the remaining answers. The clues to many of the questions are in this present volume.

1. Which bird's spring call can be described as a whistle?
2. What is a Reed Sparrow?
3. Which are usually the first and last summer visitors to arrive?
4. To which orders do the Nightjar and Wryneck belong?
5. Which birds are known as the Water Crow and the Water Sparrow?
6. What is the chief food of the Cuckoo?
7. What is a Knot?
8. Which of the shrikes winter in Britain?
9. Describe the call of the Whimbrel.
10. Give some other names for the Tawny owl.
11. What are Scapulars?
12. What is a 'Thick Knee'?
13. Name three birds which invariably lay two eggs.
14. Of the four species of wagtail, which two are summer visitors?
15. Which is the only resident British warbler?
16. What are the chief recognition features of the Lesser whitethroat?
17. Name an uncommon visiting Starling.
18. Birds eggs are of three shapes. What are they?
19. Name six birds which sing in mild weather in the New Year.
20. Name three species of winter migrants.
21. What colour are the legs of the Herring gull, Greater black-backed gull, Lesser black-backed gull, and the Common gull?
22. What are the colours on the bills of the Common tern, Arctic tern, Roseate tern, and Little tern?
23. What are the colours on the legs of the Tern species mentioned?
24. Which is the smallest falcon?
25. Name the differences between the Corn bunting and the Cirl bunting.
26. Name the differences between the Stone-chat and the Whin-chat.
27. List six birds with decurved bills.

28. Why is the Dotterel so called?
29. What is a Tit lark?
30. How many species of Owls are there in Britain?
31. What are the differences in the outward migratory times of the Cuckoo, Swift, Swallow, and House Martin?
32. Name four Doves; to which family do they belong?
33. Can you name five species of Grebe?
34. What is a summer visitor, a winter visitor, a migrant?
35. What is a Sanderling?
36. Describe the Little stint; where would you look for one?
37. Can you list eight members of the family *Corvidae*?
38. What are the differences between a Water hen and a Water rail?
39. What is a Popinjay?
40. Can you name four birds which use mud in building their nests?
41. What is the colour of the eggs of the Spotted flycatcher and Pied flycatcher?
42. What do these words mean: Couvert, Eclipse, Lores?
43. What is the largest flying bird in the world?
44. Which bird is thought to make the longest migratory flight?
46. Can you name two white gulls?
47. What is a 'Gorget'?
48. What do the following words signify: Iris, Nape, Gape?
49. Name a colour distinction between the male and female Green woodpecker.
50. Can you list four species of Skuas?
51. What are the distinguishing features of a Shore lark?
52. Can you name four birds with peculiar utterances?
53. Can you list ten species which might be expected at a reservoir in winter?
54. What is the largest British visiting Diver?
55. What is a Bufflehead?
56. Name a small bird with a long tail.
57. Can you name four species of buzzard?
58. To which bird does the collective noun 'spring' apply?
59. What is a Squib?
60. Can you name two birds, one with a long, and one with a short breeding season?
61. What is a Roller?
62. Can you list three birds which display in flight examples of hovering, gliding, and tumbling?
63. What are the differences in the colour of the male and female Hen harrier?
64. Can you list four sandpipers?
65. Can you list six warblers?
66. Name the differences between the Common swift and the Alpine swift.
67. Do you know the names of three ornithologists who have had birds named after them?

Answers to Questions
 1. The Nuthatch.
 2. The Reed bunting.
 3. Usually the Wheatear, early in March, and the Spotted flycatcher, early in May.
 4. Nightjar, order *Caprimulgyformes*, nocturnal or crepuscular birds: Wryneck order *Pasiformes*, mostly arboreal, two toes forward, and two backward.
 5. The Dipper, the Reed bunting.
 6. The larvae of species of *Lapidaptera* and *Hymonoptera*.
 7. The Knot is a greyish, plump looking wader, with shortish legs.
 8. The Great-grey Shrike.
 9. The Whimbrel – a rippling, twittering call, repeated several times.
 10. The Tawny owl, also known as the Wood and the Brown owl.
 11. The feathers covering the shoulder blades of a bird.
 12. The Stone curlew.
 13. The Swift, Woodpigeon, Nightjar.
 14. The White and Yellow wagtail.
 15. The Dartford warbler.
 16. The Lesser whitethroat is slightly smaller than the Common whitethroat, and generally greyer and darker.
 17. The Rose-coloured starling, a vagrant mainly to eastern counties.
 18. The three shapes of birds' eggs are eliptical, pear-shaped and spherical.
 19. Robin, Wren, Hedge sparrow, Skylark, Mistle thrush, Song thrush.
 20. Fieldfare, Redwing, Brambling.
 21. Herring gull and Greater Black-backed gull, pink or flesh colour legs; Lesser Black-backed gull, yellow legs; Common gull, greenish yellow legs.
 22. Common tern, bill in summer scarlet with a black tip; Arctic tern, bill red, no black tip; Roseate tern, bill black, turning red at base; Little tern, orange, black tip.
 23. Common tern, legs vermillion; Arctic tern, legs red; Roseate tern, legs red; Little tern, legs yellow.
 24. The Merlin.
 25. The Corn bunting, buffish, streaked with no white on tail; the Cirl bunting, black throat and white surround.
 26. The male Stonechat, white on neck and rusty breast; the Whinchat, dark brown cheeks, white eye stripe, white wing bar, and white on tail. The first is a resident and the second a summer visitor.
 27. Tree-creeper, Curlew, Curlew Sandpiper, Whimbrel, Dunlin, Ruff.
 28. Dotterel means dote, silly, denoting the ease with which the bird can be caught.
 29. Tit lark is another name for the Meadow pipit.
 30. Six species – Barn owl, Snowy, Little, Tawny, Short-eared, and Long-eared owls.
 31. Male Cuckoos leave (July) before the females; the young remain until

later (September). Adult Swifts and young leave together, about mid-August, stragglers later. Swallows leave September-October, adult and young, House Martins similarly.

32. Stock-dove, Ring dove (or Woodpigeon), Rock dove, Turtle dove, Family *Columbidae*.

33. Great-crested, Little, Black necked, Red necked, and Slavonian grebes.

34. A summer visitor is a species which arrives in Britain to breed, roughly from mid-March to early May; a winter visitor arrives in the autumn and early winter, remaining until February-March: a vagrant is an uncommon species – a stray arrival.

35. Sanderling, a winter visitor, but a few remain throughout the summer. It is a whitish looking wader, with dark patch on shoulders; chestnut brown above in summer, white wing bar, and white underparts. Preference for sandy shores: breeds in the arctic.

36. The Little stint *(Caldris minute)* is another Arctic breeding bird. Upper parts greyish in winter, white below; in summer rufus and black. About the size of a Dunlin.

37. Rook, Carrion and Hooded crows, Chough, Jackdaw, Magpie, Jay and Raven.

38. Water hen, or Moorhen, red bill, yellow tipped, white flank stripe. Legs and toes yellowish green: Water Rail, smaller, long red bill.

39. Popinjay is a name for the Green woodpecker.

40. Swallow, House martin, Song thrush, Ring ouzel.

41. Spotted flycatcher, eggs variable, pale greenish to bluish white, mottled with reddish spots; Pied flycatcher, eggs pale blue.

42. Couverts are feathers on the base of the wings and tail: Eclipse, the change in plumage of drakes after the breeding season: Lores, the space between the eye and the bill.

43. The Giant albatross.

44. The Arctic tern, roughly from Pole to Pole, twice a year.

45. A Tiercel is a male Hawk.

46. Glaucous gull and Common gull.

47. 'Gorget' is a colour patch on a bird's throat, prominent in some species.

48. Iris, a circular curtain around the pupil of the eye; Nape the area at the back of the neck: Gape, the wide soft mouth (mandibills) of a young bird.

49. The crimson crown of the male Green woodpecker is more conspicuous than that of the female.

50. Arctic, Long-tailed, Pomarine, and Great skuas.

51. Shore lark, a shorter tail than the skylark, black and yellow pattern around the throat: greyish on belly. The female is browner.

52. Four birds with peculiar utterances are the Grasshopper Warbler, Nightjar, Corncrake and Bittern.

53. Widgeon, Teal, Great Crested Grebe, Goosander, Smew, Mallard, Pochard, Goldeneye and Scaup.

54. The Great Northern Diver. Infrequent appearances off British coasts

October-April.

55. Bufflehead, a North American Duck, accidental to Britain.

56. The Long-tailed Tit.

57. Honey buzzard, Common, Rough-legged, Long legged.

58. Flocks of Teal.

59. A Squib is a young Wood pigeon, still in the nest.

60. Wood pigeon, long breeding season; Nightingale, a short one.

61. The Roller is a rare visitor, mostly to the east and south coasts of England. Shrike-like, with a blue head and breast and chestnut back.

62. Kestrel hovers, Albatross glides, Peewit, or Green plover tumbling flight.

63. Male Hen Harrier grey, female brown, general impression white patterned.

64. Common, Purple, Wood, and Curlew Sandpiper.

65. Garden, Willow, Grasshopper, Savi's, Marsh, Sedge Warblers.

66. Alpine Swift *(Anus melba),* a rare visitor, larger than the Common Swift *(Apus apus)* browner in colour, with a white throat, breast and belly.

67. Teminick's stint, Montagu's harrier, Richard's pipit.

Index of Species

mentioned

in this Book

SPECIES IN THIS BOOK

Bold figures indicate engravings in text